SHAKESPEARE'S
TROILUS AND CRESSIDA
AND ITS SETTING

SHAKESPEARE'S
TROILUS & CRESSIDA
AND ITS SETTING

ROBERT KIMBROUGH

HARVARD UNIVERSITY PRESS

CAMBRIDGE, MASSACHUSETTS

1964

Distributed in Great Britain
by Oxford University Press

The publication of this book has been aided
by a grant from the Hyder Edward Rollins Fund

Library of Congress Catalog Card Number 64–21243

Printed in the United States of America

TO MY WIFE
AND
TO MY PARENTS

PREFACE

CRITICS AND SCHOLARS are wont to say that not even the editors of the First Folio knew what to make of *Troilus and Cressida*. Although the assertion has almost no validity, it is a comforting, protective one to repeat: comforting, for no play by Shakespeare has received such diverse interpretation; protective, for the statement absolves one from re-examining the basic facts surrounding the play. Diversity in Shakespearean interpretation is certainly desirable, yet that concerning *Troilus and Cressida* has become confusing and contradictory because the play is approached from assumptions about its origins which are themselves widely diverse. The bias of the following study of the play and its setting is, then, frankly historical.

Two decades ago such a statement would have been seen as another shot fired in the war between the scholars and the critics, but today's student of Shakespeare has danced attendance in both camps, and feels without self-consciousness that he must try constantly to counterbalance the deadening effects of "scientific" scholarship with the invigorating effects of "pure" criticism, and to check by means of the available and ever growing mass of scholarly fact the tendency to refine criticism to airy nothing. Still, all along and in spite of disclaimers, the best work of scholars such as Hardin Craig and O. J. Campbell has been critical just as, conversely, Theodore Spencer's fine *Shakespeare and the Nature of Man* is scholarly. And it is men such as these who marked the approach to what Douglas Bush has called "the new Shakespeare" — Shakespeare recognized both as an artist and a craftsman, a man of genius working in the matter of a factual environment.

Although my intention throughout has been to shed light

on a play, perhaps a more important contribution is the suggestion of a new method for the study of Shakespeare's plays through the measuring of puzzling aspects of a given play against its sources and against analogous aspects of plays in the canon and in the competing public and private repertories. And, as do all who write on Shakespeare, I hope that my detailed analysis of *Troilus and Cressida* and its setting may bring us one small step closer to an understanding of Shakespeare's genius — yet, I keep before me as a motto what Melville said of Hawthorne: "He is immeasurably deeper than the plummet of the mere critic. For it is not the brain that can test such a man; it is only the heart. You cannot come to know greatness by inspecting it; there is no glimpse to be caught of it, except by intuition; you need not ring it, you but touch it, and you find it is gold."

In chapters II and III I have used some material from parts of articles which appeared in *PMLA* and *The Modern Language Review* and wish to thank the respective editors, the Modern Language Association, and the Modern Humanities Research Association for allowing me to repeat myself. Act, scene, and line references when plays are so divided, line or page references when they are not, are all included in the text. All quotations of Shakespeare are from the Kittredge edition published by Ginn and Company, Greg's Quarto prepared for the Shakespeare Association, and the Yale facsimile Folio; of other playwrights, from editions which are noted in the bibliography of primary sources. I have not standardized these quotations, but have eliminated the long *s*, ligatures, and those abbreviations which were indicated by superior, horizontal strokes. Because authors' names are in the text mainly for the purpose of identification of plays, I do not try to record all possible collaborators nor would I have it inferred that I have tried to establish the authorship of plays of doubtful ascription. A further attempt to eliminate end notes is the leaving unnoted of clear and general references, such as the ones to the scholars and critics mentioned above. When notes are necessary, I have not extended or qualified the presentation, but have given only the sources of quotations, sources of support for points raised, sources of judgments identical or similar to mine, and sources of counter opinion.

This decision to keep end notes to a minimum with regard to number and length stems from no desire either to slough scholarly responsibility or to appear boldly independent. Because of the nature of my study, I believe that any reader will be, at least, so generally versed in Elizabethan bibliography that he will prefer continuity to busyness, and that he easily will be able to discern the extensive debt to major writers and major trends of Shakespearean scholarship and criticism which I have accrued and here gladly acknowledge.

Other debts are not so public. Alfred Harbage was my doctoral advisor and supervised the initial version of this study; Herschel Baker also read the original manuscript and gave me helpful advice on it and many other matters; Helen C. White and Robert K. Presson encouraged me to revise and expand my thesis into a book; William Rosen and Standish Henning suggested what I might put in and what I should leave out. To each I am more grateful than I can say.

Robert Kimbrough

Madison, Wisconsin
April 1964

CONTENTS

WHY LOOKE YOU SIR, I write so plaine, and keepe that old *Decorum*, that you must of necessitie like it; mary you shall haue some now (as for example, in plaies) that will haue euery day new trickes, and write you nothing but humours: indeed this pleases the Gentlemen: but the common sort they care not for't, they know not what to make on't, they looke for good matter, they, and are not edified with such toyes . . . I care not for the Gentlemen I, let me haue good ground, no matter for the pen, the plot shall carry it.

Ben Jonson's "Anthony Munday" speaking in an addition written for a performance of *The Case is Alterd* in 1601 at Blackfriars

*I*N 1896, F. S. BOAS in *Shakspere and his Predecessors* opened his discussion of *Hamlet, Troilus and Cressida, All's Well That Ends Well,* and *Measure for Measure* with the observation that "throughout these plays we move along dim untrodden paths, and at the close our feeling is neither of simple joy nor pain; we are excited, fascinated, perplexed, for the issues raised preclude a completely satisfactory outcome, . . . and we are left to interpret their enigmas as best we may. Dramas so singular in theme and temper cannot be strictly called comedies or tragedies. We may therefore borrow a convenient phrase from the theatre of to-day and class them together as Shakspere's problem-plays." Thus was initiated the ambiguous label, "the problem plays." On the one hand, they seem to be plays which observe, examine, and comment on ethical "problems" without conclusive resolution much as the New Drama of Shaw was doing — indeed, Shaw observed in his 1898 Preface to *Plays Pleasant and Unpleasant* that in the plays mentioned by Boas we find Shakespeare "ready and willing to start at the twentieth century if the seventeenth would only let him." On the other hand, the plays are themselves "problems" if only, with the exception of *Hamlet,* because they resist easy classification: the publishers of the *Troilus and Cressida* quarto originally called the play a history because of its subject matter, then called it a comedy because of its manner of presentation, and the editors of the Folio considered the play a tragedy because it ended with the death of Hector. Thus two definitions are involved in one, and confusion has been the result. For example, W. W. Lawrence decided that *Troilus* was a comedy, dropped *Hamlet,* and discussed Shakespeare's "problem comedies"; E. M. W. Tillyard restored *Hamlet* to the group and returned to the phrase problem plays with full awareness of its ambiguity; A. P. Rossiter enlarged the group to include all of Shakespeare's middle plays; and Ernest Schanzer has just suggested that the real problem plays are *Julius Caesar, Measure for Measure,* and *Antony and Cleopatra*.[1] Lest we simply compound this confusion concerning terms and groupings I suggest we try to solve the particular aesthetic problems of the plays themselves instead of deciding by default that they are or are not generically problem plays. Once we are fairly sure what a play is like in and of itself, then we can begin to make meaningful observations regarding what it does and which other plays it resembles.

I purpose in this study, then, to subject *Troilus and Cressida* to aesthetic and historical examination in order to come as close as possible to solving the problems which the play presents when read as a piece of dramatic literature. My assumptions are that we can establish at least a working agreement concerning the nature of the play and that by examining its environment we can come to a reasonable explanation of why the play is as it is. My purpose is hardly to provide the "final word" on *Troilus,* only to prepare the ground for further revealing historical study and creative, imaginative criticism.

Certainly much of moment has come before. As can be expected, the casual observations of Johnson and Coleridge anticipate almost everything that has been written on *Troilus and Cressida* in this century when the rise of historical and new critical methods coincided with a renewal of interest in the play. Pioneers were J. H. Penniman and R. A. Small, who separately subjected the *Poetomachia* to historical analysis and found *Troilus and Cressida* only in the fringes of the battle. In 1935, Robert B. Sharpe suggested that the real War of the Theatres was between the Chamberlain's and Admiral's men and that Shakespeare wrote *Troilus* for a special performance of the play before the Queen by his company and the rival Children of the Chapel Royal on 29 December 1601, the men playing the Greeks and the boys, the Trojans; Achilles representing Cecil and Hector, Essex. Sharpe's thesis no longer is tenable in the light of Alfred Harbage's delineation of the rival theatrical traditions of Shakespeare's day, of which the *Poetomachia* was but one manifestation. Even if one cannot subscribe to the intensity of opposition which Harbage describes, no future study of the setting of Elizabethan drama can ignore his survey. Indeed, Robert Ornstein's searching analysis of Jacobean tragedy stems in part from his negative reaction to Harbage's method and thesis, as does John J. Enck's analysis of what triggered the *Poetomachia* and his suggestion of what it really was: an aesthetic "struggle about correctness based generally but not wholly on rivalries." Two other writers have been concerned with the aesthetics of drama at the turn of the century: William W. Main believes that *Troilus and Cressida* can be understood only as a kind of amalgamation or archetype of the Elizabethan repertory, 1598–1603, and Margaret Swanson Lacy believes that like other writers in the early 1600's, Shakespeare was struggling to put new wine into old bottles, trying to find a platform for new ideas within the confines of the old romance plot.[2]

Some of the important historical scholarship on *Troilus and Cressida* has been by J. S. P. Tatlock, Hyder Edward Rollins, and Robert K. Presson, who have studied the play through the comparative, historical study of its sources; by E. E. Willoughby and S. A. Tannenbaum, who in the 1930's made detailed studies of the text; by Philip Williams and Alice Walker, who in the late 1940's independently completed definitive textual analyses of the Quarto and Folio versions of the play; and by O. J. Campbell and H. B.

Charlton, who during the 1930's made important simultaneous studies of the play as a comedy. Campbell approached the play through the thesis that the outburst of literary satire in the late 1590's generally, and Ben Jonson's three "comicall satyres" particularly, worked as shaping influences on *Troilus and Cressida*. Although I think that Campbell wrenches the play to fit the thesis, my work is obviously an outgrowth of his exploration of the literary and theatrical setting of the play. Alvin Kernan and Robert C. Elliott also have acknowledged indebtedness to Campbell in their recent studies of satire, and both in turn have contributed greatly to our understanding of that literary innovation of the late 1590's and early 1600's, in print and on the stage.[3]

Charlton's work treats *Troilus* as an important keystone in the growth and development of Shakespearean comedy. Because he felt that the play is pivotal or transitional with relation to the canon, Charlton, like so many others, was content to pass by the problem of *Troilus* taken by itself in order to talk about the larger question of Shakespeare's mind and art midway through his career. Ironically, this kind of treatment has led to some of the most revealing criticism on the play: Theodore Spencer, E. M. W. Tillyard, Virgil Whitaker, and Robert Ornstein teach us much about *Troilus* although their main concern is Shakespeare and his stage.

G. Wilson Knight, on the other hand, tends to ignore Shakespeare as he focuses directly on *Troilus*; moreover, he reads the play so closely that it is distorted in his criticism as a piece of dramatic literature and becomes a philosophical text which argues that the life of intuition as illustrated by Troilus and the Trojans has true "beauty and worth" while the life of pragmatic reason as illustrated by Ulysses and the Greeks reveals "the bestial and stupid elements of man." D.

A. Traversi and L. C. Knights, openly indebted to the thesis and method of Knight, elucidate nuances in the text, but Albert Gérard's recent reading of the play as the story of "the victory of Greek materialism over Trojan idealism" shows both the pervasive, repetitive influence of Knight and that critics as well as scholars can be blind to the poetic, dramatic, and theatrical logic of a play. Others, such as David C. Kaula and Richard C. Harrier, try to marry the school of Campbell to the school of Knight, but most essays on the play have followed the suggestions of Shaw, Boas, and W. W. Lawrence and defined it as a problem play; however, the nature of the problem and its inferred solution are not always the same. We would be hard pressed not to agree, for example, with A. S. Knowland that the play is a study in "the way things happen." [4]

Knowland's conclusion provides a useful clew to what has happened in twentieth-century criticism of Shakespeare. Since James and Joyce we have finally recognized that the novel, with its discursive treatment of the materials of life as a human comedy, is a major, highly complex art form, and because we have always recognized that Shakespeare is the consummate artist, we tend to treat his plays as texts to be read — which, of course, they are and always have been. But they appeared in print only because Shakespeare established himself as a successful writer for the theater. One would have to be very dull indeed to quarrel with the brilliant work of Wilson Knight and his followers. They have done much to show us the extent and complexity of Shakespeare's genius. The danger is, as Allardyce Nicoll reminds us, that just fascination with Shakespeare can blind us to the individual qualities of the separate plays. [5]

In the case of *Troilus and Cressida* the danger is greatest because, as Swinburne observed in *A Study of Shakespeare* (1880), "alike in its most palpable perplexities and in its most patent splendours, this political and philosophic and poetic problem, this hybrid and hundred-faced and hydra-headed prodigy, at once defies and derides all definitive comment." As a result, "this wonderful play, one of the most admirable among all the works of Shakespeare's immeasurable and unfathomable intelligence, . . . must always hold its natural high place among the most admired." At the same time, he concluded, it will always "in all probability be also, and as naturally, the least beloved of all." This is but one way of saying that as effective drama *Troilus* is a failure.

To say that Shakespeare wrote a bad play does not necessitate our saying, as T. S. Eliot did of *Hamlet*, that it is not a great work of art. The leisure of the study provides opportunities for kinds of response which the theater does not, and what may be blurred and muted in the latter can be puzzled out and emphasized in the former. The worthy amount of sophisticated literature which *Troilus and Cressida* has evoked is sufficient proof that as a text the play is a success. Still a spade is not a heart, and a parallel appeal to history would seem to bear out the conclusion of my analysis of *Troilus* as drama — it does not play well. In chapter II I shall try to prove that *Troilus* appeared only briefly in the Chamberlain's repertory during the season of 1601–1602. Until now the record of Dryden's adaptation affords the only stage history of the play in the seventeenth century, and, in spite of the general increase in popularity of Shakespeare's plays, his *Troilus* was not revived in the eighteenth century, although Dryden's played briefly at Drury Lane.[6] Early in the nineteenth century Kemble cut, rearranged, and cast the play, but did not produce it, and another adaptation of the play, dated 1810, survives in the British Museum. But no other efforts toward revival have been discovered, and this theatrical indifference is an impressive kind of unrecorded criticism, the nature of which is typified by the two dormant cut, rearranged, and rewritten manuscript texts of the play. Finally, in 1898 in Germany and in 1905 in England, there occur the first recorded performances, and there have been so few that the editors of the *Variorum* were able to attempt to list every performance in the world up to 1948.[7] But in the 1950's and 1960's the Stratford companies in England, Canada, and America, the Old Vic, numerous summer festivals, and various academic groups have produced the play. This sudden outburst clearly is related to the times in which we live, directors and students finding a mirror for present doubt, confusion, and sense of crumbling values in Shakespeare's world of the play. But I know of no production that has not been based on a cut or tampered text as we know it, and most productions have been highly stylized, usually emphasizing the decadence of both camps and the love story. The "purest" production was that which opened the new Loeb Drama Center at Harvard in the fall of 1960, but the reviews all praise the theater and the actors, not the play.[8]

What I am trying to show is how and why the play is not good drama even though it contains a dazzling variety of characters, complicated plotting, and a medley of profound themes. Such an attempt, one may charge, and justly so, examines the frame but ignores the picture, emphasizes the negative at the expense of the positive, points out weakness instead of excellence, is, in short, perverse. My only rejoinder is that I am simply trying to see the play as it really is, good and bad together, and that the attempt necessitates the redressing of an imbalance, for the play has been treated as if it were closet drama. (In fact, Donald Stauffer in *Shakespeare's World of Images* even called it that.) As a result critical endeavor has been more concerned with themes and language and characterizations than it has with the total dramatic image or structure of the play. The eye not held, the mind is free to roam. The text, to be sure, is primarily and ultimately important, but full understanding of it demands the exploration of context.

In chapter II, I sketch the particular theatrical atmosphere out of which *Troilus and Cressida* springs in order to present my hypothesis: in 1601 Shakespeare attempted a play that embraced attributes of both the new drama of the private theaters and old drama of the public theaters; he attempted, in short, to combine "new trickes" and "old *Decorum*." Because he turned for his play to the "matter of Troy," I examine in chapter III the nature of the Trojan literature, emphasizing how it would appear to an Elizabethan artist. Once these basic quantities are established, I move in chapter IV to the play itself and attempt to isolate, through an analysis of its plot, the three particular areas which yield critical problems: the love story, the Trojan story, and the Greek story. These, then, are further analyzed in three successive chapters (V, VI, and VII) and the problems which arise out of them are measured against analogous aspects of the preceding Shakespearean canon and the extant plays presented in London from 1598 to 1603 in order to obtain a critical perspective from the personal and commercial points of view. I was tempted to enlarge this contextual approach to include the social and political backgrounds of 1598 to 1603, but resisted. Tucker Brooke, G. B. Harrison, and Paul N. Siegel have covered the area about as well as can be done.[9] There is, furthermore, little common ground between the events in a play and the thoughts in a poet's mind regarding actual events in life. Within the canon, however, and in the competing repertories we have a reliable basis for comparison and contrast: the aesthetic constant of drama. Finally, in chapter VIII, through a synthesis and summary of the preceding facts and observations, I hope to convince the reader that Shakespeare tried in *Troilus and*

Cressida to stem the tide of customers being drawn away from the public theaters in 1600 and 1601 by the newly re-established chorister companies, but was unwilling to write a play in full imitation of the new private repertory; the conventions and traditions of his own theater were too strong to be abandoned casually. The result was that *Troilus and Cressida* did not evolve as effective drama, as "good theater." But the hand of genius is everywhere to be seen in it and Shakespeare profited greatly from exercising his talents outside his customary modes. Indeed no one who works with the play can help being drawn to the conclusion that it is most important in the development of his art. Because my work does try to isolate Shakespeare's intentions and tends to ignore his achievements, I indulge in conjecture in a short epilogue regarding the positive dramatic values of the play and its effect on Shakespeare, then go on to suggest how it provides us with evidence about the evolving nature of the Elizabethan theater.

CHAPTER II · THE THEATRICAL
ORIGINS OF THE PLAY

*L*ONDON EXPERIENCED a theatrical boom in the late 1590's. After they moved to the Bankside in 1597 when The Theatre was closed, the Chamberlain's Men earned sufficient money even while paying rent at the Curtain to be able to finance the building of their own theater. In the fall of 1599 Philip Henslowe had to face not only the competition of the old company at the new Globe, but also that offered by the company of children who had been reinstated as players at Paul's. Nevertheless, he and Edward Alleyn had been doing so well with the Admiral's Men that they were able to move their enterprise into the rapidly growing and prospering area north of London proper. When they opened in the fall of 1600 at their newly built Fortune, still more competition was on the scene: the chorister Children of the Chapel Royal were now playing at the Burbage-owned Blackfriars Theatre. The Curtain and the Rose, in addition to various inns such as the Boar's Head, were available for the intermittent activity of Pembroke's, Derby's, Oxford's, and Worcester's men.[1]

This sudden enlargement of theatrical production must have created a seller's market for writers, for the various companies certainly wanted fresh material in order to draw and retain for themselves new and regular audiences. It has been suggested by O. J. Campbell and others that the Bishop's ban on John Marston's satires in June of 1599 drove him into the theaters; however, there is a stronger possibility that Marston turned dramatist simply because the theaters were looking for writers. That Paul's was opening saved him from the disgrace of having to write for the "common players." Ben Jonson, too, welcomed at this time the chance to write for a private company; when Blackfriars opened he was able to escape from the double disgrace of having a failure in *Every Man out of his Humour* at the Globe and of having to patch up old plays for Henslowe.

In *Histrio-mastix* and in an addition to *The Case is Alterd*, their earliest extant work for their respective private theaters, Marston and Jonson implied that ten pounds should be the price paid for a play.[2] To ask for almost double the going rate would have been foolhardy had not the economics of the theatrical world suggested some real possibility of their getting it. And from what Rosencrantz and Guildenstern tell Hamlet about the boys' carrying it away we may infer that Marston and Jonson were bargaining from a strong position.

With the theaters competing hard for audiences, it is not surprising that a minor civil war broke out among the writers competing for the producers' pounds. Alfred Harbage has indicated that there are various important implications in the War of the Theatres beyond the commercial skirmishes between houses, the personal exchanges between writers, and the "cuffs" between poets and players: it was "in addition . . . symptomatic of deep-seated tensions, involving class antagonisms, rival moral philosophies, and, in a fashion, even the issue of ancients *versus* moderns."[3] The important thing here is that the very existence of a *Poetomachia* affords significant evidence that the theatrical scene in London from 1598 to 1603 was highly competitive and shifting. After Queen Elizabeth's death and the long plague of 1603 the scene was more settled — Jonson, for example, was writing for the King's Men — but during this period of adjustment writers were intensely aware of the work of others, each hoping that he would quickly find what modes, methods, and motifs would lead to some sort of regular and stable "box-office."[4]

THE THEATRICAL SCENE, 1598–1603

Prologues and inductions were designed to prepare an audience not only for the particular story that was to follow, but also for the manner in which the play was to be developed.[5] Likewise, epilogues took on more than the function of eliciting applause; they afforded the author a means of evaluating his success in giving his public what he thought it wanted. The epilogue to *All's Well That Ends Well*, for example, not only asks warmly and humbly for applause, but promises to repay present approval "with strife to please you, day exceeding day" (V. iii. 338). Even Feste's epilogue to *Twelfth Night*, although organic to the play and far-reaching in its evocations, concludes with recognition of the specific relationship between the players and the audience:

> A great while ago the world begun,
>   With hey, ho, the wind and the rain;
> But that's all one, our play is done,
>   And we'll strive to please you every day.   (V. i. 414–417)

Although Rosalind's epilogue to *As You Like It* seems only to ask good-naturedly for applause, the first half betrays an artistic self-consciousness on Shakespeare's part: "It is not the fashion to see the lady the epilogue; but it is no more unhandsome than to see the lord the prologue . . . 'tis true that a good play needs no epilogue . . . I cannot insinuate with you in the behalf of a good play!" And the epilogue to *Henry V* is spoken with the same self-effacement of the various prologues within that play:

> Thus far, with rough and all-unable pen,
>   Our bending author hath pursu'd the story,
> In little room confining mighty men,
>   Mangling by starts the full course of their glory.

Ben Jonson, in a prologue to *Every Man in his Humour* written later but designed, in the opinion of Herford and Simpson, "to retain the atmosphere of 1598," [6] ridiculed the public stage through his remarks on *Henry V*, but Shakespeare's
artistic self-consciousness here reveals his own awareness of
the active theatrical scene of 1598 to 1603, and his tone stands
in marked contrast to that of Jonson in the last words of
the epilogue to *Cynthia's Revels*: "*By God 'tis good, and if
you lik't, you may.*" [7]

Because of the modern image of the artist as one who lives
and works uncontaminated by commerce and convention,
we do not often recall that Shakespeare owed much of his
long and continuous success to his ability to ride prevailing
theatrical and literary winds. He wrote in the Marlovian
vein when bombasting out a blank verse was the style,
chronicle history plays when they were in vogue, a Senecan
revenge tragedy in emulation of the successful *The Spanish
Tragedy*, and comedies that could rival the courtly plays
of Lyly. Furthermore *Venus and Adonis* and *Lucrece* were
written in the appropriate, fashionable genres of 1593 and
1594. But this awareness of fashions does not carry implications of blind conformity; it merely shows a willingness
on Shakespeare's part to try to meet and overcome the
particular commercial and artistic challenges of the day.

Certainly one of the important literary developments of
the late 1590's was the sudden outburst of satire as a separate
genre.[8] Just as Shakespeare had incorporated then-fashionable
sonnets into *The Two Gentlemen of Verona* and *Romeo
and Juliet* when they would enhance the aura of romantic
love, at the turn of the century he seems to have used the
vogue of satire in order to heighten the effect of his drama.
For example, Claudio in *Much Ado About Nothing* denounces Hero's seeming dishonesty in rich and sensuous
terms:

> you are more intemperate in your blood
> Than Venus, or those pamp'red animals,
> That rage in savage sensuality,   (IV. i. 60–62)

and in his disillusionment he begins to doubt the divinity of beauty and the chastity of women. When he shouts in a Juvenalian rage, "Out on the seeming! I will write against it," he allies himself with the contemporary "angry young men" of London: Donne, Hall, and Marston.

At the end of the same play, "Benedick, the married man," shows that he has changed his views on marriage, and that other detractors can have no influence on him: "a college of wit-crackers cannot flout me out of my humour. Dost thou think I care for a satire or an epigram? No. If a man will be beaten with brains, 'a shall wear nothing handsome about him. In brief, since I do purpose to marry, I will think nothing to any purpose that the world can say against it" (V. iv. 101–108). What Claudio would have written, the new Benedick would have ignored. Jaques, in *As You Like It*, however, would have devoured it avidly, for he is presented as a practicing satirist.[9]

Shakespeare's picture of the satiric vogue is balanced, the chastisement which Jaques receives from the Duke Senior and Olivia's rebuke of Malvolio being similar to other contemporary reactions against the excesses of satire.[10] Hamlet's justification of his extreme diction and detraction in the closet scene is completely Juvenalian: *difficile est satyram non scribere*. Earlier, he has been reading a "satirical rogue" (II. ii. 198) apparently related to Benedick's "wit-crackers" and Troilus' "stubborn critics" who damn all women when only some are unfaithful (V. ii. 131) because the writer summarily dismisses old men as bundles of physical and mental decrepitude. Hamlet holds "it not honesty to have it thus set down," even though his own satiric bent is further shown in his comments on Osric, the courtly "water-fly" (V. ii). Fastidious courtiers always had been fair game for English satirists; Faulconbridge's mockery in *King John* is quite typical of the generalized manner in which they were treated. But O. J. Campbell has shown that Touchstone's lengthy descriptions of fatuous courtly customs in *As You Like It* was the beginning of this Shakespearean adoption of the methods of the new literary satire in his plays, and that each of Shakespeare's plays from 1598 to 1603 has at least one satirical spokesman in it. Furthermore, Campbell and Alvin Kernan have shown how the plays of Jonson and Marston that were being introduced in the newly opened chorister playhouses have a close generic relationship to the products of the literary satirists.[11]

That Shakespeare was aware of the commercial threat which these new enterprises offered is quite apparent from the conversation which Hamlet holds with Rosencrantz and Guildenstern concerning the players. It is also equally apparent that he was aware of the kind of play being offered by his new opposition. Corporal Nym's use of the word "humour" in every speech in *Henry V* is clearly a general ribbing of Chapman's and Jonson's use of the pseudoesoteric humour psychology in their plays for the public theaters during 1596 to 1598; hence, it is particularly noteworthy that in *The Merry Wives of Windsor* Nym is no longer merely an ignorant clown, but tries to act the part of a great detractor of the human scene.[12] In spite of this mockery through Nym of Jonson's latest dramatic method, Shakespeare seems to have seriously used Jonsonian techniques in constructing *Twelfth Night.*[13] But when we recall that Sir Andrew Aguecheek is a very real, appealing character in addition to being an ignorant, foppish gull, and that Malvolio is the recipient of more satiric correction than he is able to administer, we need not fall into the naïve assumption that Shakespeare was a servile imitator.

In addition to its general, satiric laughter at fools, and its use of cynical observers of the human scene, another prominent characteristic of the new drama was its emphasis on lust and the demands of the flesh. Sir John Falstaff's plan to cuckold the citizen husbands of *The Merry Wives of Windsor* has all the earmarks of the fashionable comedy of the private theaters: he intends to "make love to Ford's wife" who, he says, has given him "the leer of invitation" and who "has all the rule of her husband's purse"; he believes that Page's wife also has cast a lecherous eye on him, and she "bears the purse too." He concludes, "I will be cheaters to them both, and they shall be exchequers to me" (I. iii. passim). However, the Mistresses Ford and Page are from the beginning aware of his "wicked fire of lust" (II. i. 69), and Mistress Page speaks for both ladies:

> Hang him, dishonest varlet! We cannot misuse him enough.
> We'll leave a proof by that which we will do,
> Wives may be merry, and yet honest too.   (IV. ii. 104–106)

Although James Burbage built the second Blackfriars in 1596, the Chamberlain's (King's) Men did not extend their operations to the city proper until 1608 or 1609.[14] If Shakespeare's company early entertained the idea of trying to capture more of the fashionable trade, they did not decide to make an all-out attack with *The Merry Wives of Windsor*, for its philosophy was not fully geared to coterie taste. One reason is not far to seek. The way in which the phrase "all's well that ends well" is incorporated into the dialogue of *All's Well* indicates an awareness of a coterie convention, but Lafew's exclamation, "Lustick! as the Dutchman says," (II. iii. 47) is a reference to *The Weakest Goeth to the Wall* (ll. 943–946), which was currently being played publicly by Oxford's Men. Shakespeare knew full well that his competition in the years 1598 to 1603 came from the public stages as well as from the private houses. Nevertheless, I propose that in the middle of these years of intense rivalry, Shakespeare decided or was asked to attempt a coterie approach to the writing of a public play and did so in *Troilus and Cressida.*

THE PLACE AND DATE OF FIRST PERFORMANCE

Proof of such an hypothesis must rest initially on a demonstration that *Troilus and Cressida* was written for and was presented publicly by the Chamberlain's Men in 1601. Actually, the earliest established date for *Troilus and Cressida* is 7 February 1603, at which time the Stationers' Company entered "in Full Court" permission to James Roberts "to print when he hath gotten sufficient aucthority for yt. The booke of Troilus and Cresseda as yt is acted by my lo: Chamberlens Men." [15] That this is Shakespeare's play is based on the double assumption that his *Troilus and Cressida* can be dated at least this early and that his company would not have had two plays on the same topic at the same time. But another entry in the Register tends to clear up any possible doubts, for on 28 January 1609, Bonian and Walley announced that they were licensed to publish a "booke called The History of Troylus and Cressida," [16] which they later described on their title page as "THE/ Historie of Troylus/ and Cresseida./ *As it was acted by the Kings Maiesties/* seruants at the Globe./ *Written by* William Shakespeare" (sig. A). Before the entire edition was distributed, a new title page was substituted, which read "THE/ Famous Historie of/ Troylus *and* Cresseid./ *Excellently expressing the beginning/* of their loues, with the conceited wooing/ of *Pandarus* Prince of *Licia./ Written by* William Shakespeare" (sig. ¶). Moreover, a preface emphasizing Shakespeare's authorship was added which called *Troilus and Cressida* "*a new play, neuer stal'd with the Stage, neuer clapperclawd with the palmes of the vulger, and yet passing full of the palme comicall; for it is a birth of your braine, that neuer undertooke any thing comicall, vainely"* (sig. ¶₂).

In light of this 1609 preface, some scholars have concluded that *Troilus and Cressida* was never acted, even though the Roberts entry of 1603 seems on the most conservative grounds to be sufficient testimony that it was. Furthermore, the Stationers' Register provides material for two reinforcing deductions. That Roberts' request for copyright was made in "Full Court" is unusual and the reason for it remains unexplained. That permission was given only under the condition that he receive "sufficient aucthority" before printing is generally conceded to indicate that this was a blocking entry.[17] Yet two obvious questions with regard to stage history may be asked: would not a full court hearing make it less possible for a false claim that "yt is acted" to have slipped by unchallenged? and would the Chamberlain's Men block an unacted play?

C. J. Sisson has recently presented evidence that makes the first question quite pertinent. His discussion of "The Laws of Elizabethan Copyright: the Stationers' View"[18] clearly shows that hearings by the "Full Court" received careful attention and were occasions of open debate, not of routine review. The second question is answered by the fact that Thomas Middleton openly parodied *Troilus and Cressida* in 1602.

Richard H. Barker is the latest of several scholars who have pointed out numerous imitations and parodies of Shakespeare in Middleton's *The Family of Love*, a play which Barker believes "can scarcely be dated much later than 1602."[19] Because Middleton, as Barker notes, was one of a group of writers who were producing "plays that very directly reflected the intellectual currents of the day" it is not surprising to find that he would take note of Shake-

speare's defense of traditional concepts and commonplaces
in Ulysses' eloquent discourse on the philosophic necessity
for degree and order in any microcosm of the great macrocosm. Ulysses says in part:

> O, when degree is shak'd,
> Which is the ladder to all high designs,
> Then enterprise is sick! How could communities,
> Degrees in schools and brotherhoods in cities,
> Peaceful commerce from dividable shores,
> The primogenity and due of birth,
> Perogative of age, crowns, sceptres, laurels,
> But by degree, stand in authentic place?
> Take but degree away, untune that string,
> And hark what discord follows!
>
> .   .   .   .
>
> Then everything includes itself in power,
> Power into will, will into appetite;
> And appetite, an universal wolf,
> So doubly seconded with will and power,
> Must make perforce an universal prey,
> And last eat up himself.   (I. iii. 101–124)

This speech certainly must have been ringing in Middleton's ear when he wrote the following lines for the satiric
Dryfat. Dryfat, disguised as a "moral proctor," says that if
the Family of Love is not suppressed, "each man's copyhold
will become freehold, specialties will turn to generalities,
and so from unity to parity, from parity to plurality, and
from plurality to universality; their wives, the only ornaments of their houses, and of all their wares, goods, and
chattel[s], the chief moveables, will be made common"
(V. iii. 192–201).

This parody would have had no point had not *Troilus
and Cressida* been acted, and, indeed, acted before 1602.
Actually, a date of late 1601 is logical for *Troilus* because

the "Prologue arm'd . . . not in confidence/Of author's pen or actor's voice" is probably both a particular reference to Jonson's armed prologue to his *Poetaster* and a general reference to the War of the Theatres with its "cuffs" between poets and players. *Poetaster* is dated about June 1601; *Satiromastix*, about August 1601; and Jonson's "Apologeticall Dialogue" written for *Poetaster* may have been spoken in December 1601.[20] The prologue to *Troilus* would have had little point, then, before June or after December.

That the prologue and the play were written at the same time seems clear from internal evidence. Abbie Findlay Potts has suggested the thesis that "Shakespeare carefully studied *Cynthia's Revels*, 1600 [o.s.] and the *Poetaster*, 1601" before writing *Troilus and Cressida*.[21] Because her evidence is based on similar but random words and phrases, she only tentatively suggests that Shakespeare "was slyly poking fun at certain scenes in *Cynthia's Revels*." But she overlooked one passage which is a perfect parody of Jonson's style and ideas.[22] Alexander, Cressida's page, describes Ajax: "This man, lady, hath robb'd many beasts of their particular additions. He is as valiant as the lion, churlish as the bear, slow as the elephant; a man into whom nature hath so crowded humours that his valour is crush'd into folly, his folly sauced with discretion . . ." (and so on for eight more lines, I. ii. 18–31). When we put beneath this a page's description of Crites who is Jonson's spokesman in *Cynthia's Revels* if not his *persona*, it is obvious that Shakespeare was having fun at Jonson's expense: "A creature of most perfect and diuine temper. One, in whom the humours and elements are peaceably met, without emulation of precedencie: he is neyther to phantastikely melancholy, too slowly phlegmaticke, too lightly sanguine, or too rashly cholericke, but in all, so composde & order'd, as it is cleare, *Nature* went about some ful worke, she did more then make a man, when

she made him . . ." (and so on for fifteen more lines,
II. iii. 122–145). If *Troilus and Cressida* contained a "purge"
of Jonson by Shakespeare it would have to be in Alexander's
speech, even though Ajax himself is certainly not a portrait
of Jonson and the authors of 2 *The Return from Parnassus*
clearly refer in their play to *Satiromastix*.[23] Still what is pertinent is the evidence that *Troilus and Cressida* was written
and produced as the War of the Theatres of 1599 to 1602
was reaching its climax, and, if the statement in the Stationers' Register implies current stage activity, that *Troilus
and Cressida* remained in the Chamberlain's repertory for
at least a year.

Peter Alexander has argued, however, that production
was private and that the play was commissioned by one of
the Inns of Court to be performed only once.[24] Alexander's
thesis was worked out mainly to explain how Bonian and
Walley were able to obtain from private sources and print
against *"the grand possessors wills"* (Quarto, sig. ¶2v) a
copy of the play which the consensus of scholars feels must
have been a "literary" one, one which had been made from
either the author's foul papers or the playhouse copy for
the purpose of reading, not producing, the play. In general
rebuttal Alfred Harbage and T. W. Baldwin have shown
how economically infeasible such a commissioning would
have been from the point of view of an Inn.[25] Furthermore,
Shakespeare, as a shareholder in his own company, surely
did not take time away from profitable endeavor to write
and sell a new play for the students' own production. Even
if he had — and the price would have been high — and had
the students put on the play themselves, the cost still would
have been much more than simply buying a performance
of a play in one of the repertories of any of London's numerous private and public companies.[26] But above all, even if
Troilus was written for, sold to, or performed before or by

one of the Inns, we can be sure that the "literary" version
of the play was *not* provided for the occasion simply because
Pandarus' rhyming remarks at the close of III. ii and at
the end of the play clearly indicate public origins. His bawdy
tone may or may not have been appropriate to such an occasion, but the addresses to maidens, bawds, and panders were
not.[27] Thus all positive evidence indicates that *Troilus and
Cressida* was first performed publicly late in 1601.

THE TWO VERSIONS

The bibliographical questions surrounding the Quarto
and Folio are interesting in and of themselves, and have
been thoroughly aired.[28] What is of particular importance
here is the evidence that there were two versions of Shakespeare's play available to the printers, the "literary" manuscript which is the basis of the Quarto, and a playhouse copy
or even the foul papers which were used to "correct" a copy
of the Quarto for use as the copy-text for the Folio. If the
Folio does indeed embrace readings from the playhouse
copy, it would seem that the original version included the
final dismissal of Pandarus at the end of V. iii, the last
scene in Troy, and closed with Troilus' shouted defiance of
the Greeks. Although the date of revision cannot be established, its purpose is clear: to emphasize, in the words of
the second title page of the Quarto, "the conceited wooing/
of *Pandarus* Prince of *Licia*."

Because the Folio is a conflated text we can never be entirely sure what the original version of the play was like,[29]
but the existing evidence would indicate that it had an emphasis which ran counter to that of the revision. The Folio,
and supposedly the underlying manuscript, has Aeneas cap
his pledge to Troilus that he will not tell anyone about the
assignation with Cressida, "The secrets of nature/ Have not
more gift in taciturnity" (IV. ii. 74–75); yet the Quarto (and

only Pope, Johnson, Malone, and Alice Walker's New Cambridge edition) reads "the secrets of neighbor *Pandar*/ Haue not more guift in taciturnitie." The first form is in keeping with an heroic, noble vein which runs throughout the play; the second version emphasizes an equally apparent smiling, smirking attitude in the work and is in keeping with a version which would end not with Troilus but with Pandarus. It would seem that Shakespeare was not sure which vein would please the more because the epilogue of the second version was framed in part to help him decide.

When the decision was made to point up the role of Pandarus and the plot of which he is the manipulator, his dismissal was removed from the logical context of Ilium before the battle (V. iii) in order to bring him on stage illogically after the battle so that he might speak an epilogue. After Troilus labels him pander, Pandarus tries to blunt the abruptness of the dismissal first by mumbling about his aged, aching bones, as he had been doing in the last scene in Troy while Troilus read his letter from Cressida. Then, he tries to generalize his situation as the lot of life, and finally seeks escape from responsibility for the disastrous outcome of the love plot by ridiculing Troilus and Cressida through the lines of a light, lewd song:

> Full merrily the humblebee doth sing
> Till he hath lost his honey and his sting;
> And being once subdu'd in armed tail,
> Sweet honey and sweet notes together fail.   (V. x. 41–44)

After a prose application of this to his own situation, for the first time, except for an earlier couplet (III. ii. 219–220), Pandarus speaks in verse — indeed in rhymed verse. The change breaks the decorum of his character, for the couplets bounce along, whereas Pandarus usually stumbles along in his aged, prattling manner:

As many as be here of Panders' Hall,
Your eyes, half out, weep out at Pandar's fall;
Or if you cannot weep, yet give some groans,
Though not for me, yet for your aching bones.
Brethren and sisters of the hold-door trade,
Some two months hence my will shall here be made.
It should be now, but that my fear is this,
Some galled goose of Winchester would hiss.
Till then I'll sweat and seek about for eases,
And at that time bequeath you my diseases.   (V. x. 48–57)

This speech has nothing really new in it. Pandarus previously had assumed his mantle as the prototype of procurers, had complained of sickness, and had shown neither a serious nor chaste mind. But the direct address in rhyme to the procurers in the audience at the expense of the prostitutes adds a discomforting dimension to the speech. The audience which had felt so superior to and removed from the characters now turned its attention on itself, wondering whom among the spectators were being addressed and mocked.

Viewed in the light of the kinds of epilogue in the canon, Alfred Harbage finds that "it is difficult to imagine Shakespeare writing this epilogue on *any* occasion." Still, he agrees that all evidence leads to the conclusion that Pandarus' speech was designed for "regular performance at the Globe during or just after the years of *Histrio-mastix, Cynthia's Revels, Poetaster,* and *Satiromastix*." [30] What Pandarus says clearly suggests that his address was meant for a public audience; yet the way in which he says it gives a final emphasis to a lethargic, lecherous vein running through the play, a vein having its closest analogy to the atmosphere of coterie plays. While the matter of *Troilus and Cressida* was old and popular, the manner was new and fashionable.

CHAPTER III · THE LITERARY ORIGINS: THE "MATTER OF TROY"

*T*ROILUS AND CRESSIDA is "a dramatization of part of a translation into English of the French translation of a Latin imitation of an old French expansion of a Latin epitome of a Greek romance." In this way Gilbert Highet in *The Classical Tradition* traces Shakespeare's play back to the allegedly "eyewitness" anti-Trojan account of the war by one Dictys, which scholars date from the fourth century. Dictys' account was countered by the anti-Greek "true" eyewitness narrative of one Dares which was miraculously "discovered" in the fifth century, and the work of both was combined and expanded in verse by Benoît around 1160. Benoît in turn was paraphrased in a Latin prose "history" by Guido delle Colonne in 1287, which was adapted and translated back into French by Raoul Lefèvre (1464), who, finally, was translated by William Caxton (1474). But this line of descent accounts for only one probable source of the play. Boccaccio abstracted the story of Troilus and Cressida as it had been elaborated by Benoît and Guido, and, backed by Chaucer, started it in a parallel descent. Henryson fearlessly completed Chaucer's tale by showing Cressida forsaken by Diomedes, turned prostitute, inflicted with leprosy, and reduced to beggary, but Lydgate and Caxton were not so bold, referring the reader to Chaucer for the tale of the lovers, preferring to concentrate on the story of the siege. In addition to this immediate family of medieval works specifically on Troy and the lovers, Shakespeare in selecting a manner and method of treating "the matter of Troy" would have had available for general and specific reference Homer, Vergil, and Ovid as well as Elizabethan rhetoric and emblem books and the minor analogous work of his contemporaries.

If Shakespeare used immediate sources, they were probably Caxton, Chaucer, and Homer, who provide most of the details that appear in his play.[1] Not only were they the main "authorities" on Troy, but they were also readily available. Thomas Creede issued a new edition of Caxton's *The Recuyell of the Historyes of Troye* in 1596 (and again in 1607); Thomas Speght offered the works of Chaucer (which included Henryson) both in 1598 and 1602; and Chapman translated *Seaven Bookes of the Iliades* (I, II, and VI to XI) and *Achilles Shield* (XVIII) in 1598. Moreover, Shakespeare could have received hints from his competition and, in fact, he may even have been called upon to marshal his knowledge of Troy not only because of the current commercial capital being made on this always popular material by the publishers, but also by the players. In the summer of 1596 the Admiral's Men gave five performances of a play called "troye"; in the spring of 1599, Henslowe paid Chettle and Dekker for work on the play called "troyless & creseda"; and the fragment of the Admiral's plot of a play about Troy and the lovers must be dated from 1598 to 1602.[2] Whether or not this plot is "troye" reworked, the Chettle-Dekker play, or a third one, Henslowe from 1596 to 1602 was careful to have ready a play on Troy. Furthermore, in 1599 the Admiral's Men played the anonymous *Agamemnon, Troy's Revenge, Orestes' Furies*, and a two-part play on Brutus, the son of Ascanius.[3]

This last play should serve to remind us that these publications and plays are not merely diverse popular and esoteric items; they have a unity under the thesis of Geoffrey of Monmouth, reinforced by Tudor historiography, that Brutus, the grandson of Aeneas, founded Britain. As a result, the story of Troy as well as the *Aeneid* were among the

annals of Elizabethan England. What we separate into myths
and facts, cultures and nations, chronicles and literature,
periods and trends, were to the Elizabethans simply the
matter of "history." Thus, it is not surprising that, according to J. S. P. Tatlock, "no traditional story was so popular
in the Elizabethan Age as that of the siege of Troy and some
of its episodes"; [4] in many ways it portrayed the birth of
the British nation. This material — uneven, full of variety
and contradictions, yet sanctified as history [5] — might seem
unmanageable for the purposes of art. Parts of it and traditions within it could be used separately, but to epitomize it
successfully should have seemed almost impossible. Nevertheless, Shakespeare made the attempt and a survey first of
the general nature of the artistic raw materials which were
available to him in literature and in the theater, and then
of his prior use of the material in the canon will shed light
on the concerns and problems which evolved with the actual
writing of *Troilus and Cressida.*

THE "MATTER OF TROY" IN LITERATURE
AND THE THEATER

From his earliest schooling Shakespeare surely knew
Chaucer if only by reputation. But even if he read Chaucer's
Troilus and Criseyde it was with a double handicap: he
never knew Chaucer as a deft manipulator of metrics, rhyme,
and diction, and he knew *Troilus* with Henryson's *Testament of Cresseid* appended. Hence, we should be careful not
to confuse our reading of Chaucer with Shakespeare's. I
should think that many subtleties of characterization and
interior monologue would have been lost to Shakespeare
because of textual degeneration and because of the contro-
verting influence on Chaucer's narrative of the "epilogue"
full of disease and divine retribution. It may be well for us
to recognize with M. C. Bradbrook that "Chaucer's narra-

tive is an inward one," [6] but I doubt that Shakespeare could have experienced it through empathic projection.

Furthermore, to have been drawn to the characters Shakespeare would have had to divorce them from all association with their sixteenth-century stereotypes. Hyder Rollins has shown in detail how Troilus and Cressida had become flattened out into popular symbols for steadfastness and inconstancy in love.[7] His illustrations from ballads, lyrics, plays, and long poems are exhaustive and fully convincing. Indeed, the pervasiveness of the identification of Cressida with falsity was so great that it created a dilemma for George Whetstone. Needing to point a warning in *The Rocke of Regard* against loose women he betrays the fact that he used Cressida's name only because he could think of no other moral tag: "The inconstancie of Cressid is so readie in every mans mouth, . . . nevertheless, . . . her beggarie after braverie, her loathsome leprosie after lively beautie, her wretched age after wanton youth, and her perpetuall infamie after violent death, are worthy notes (for others heede) to be remembred" (p. 35).

An interesting side development to this reduction of Troilus and Cressida to the status of popular proverb is the superior, mocking attitude displayed toward them in literature more sophisticated than ballads and the work of such as Turbervile and Whetstone. In the anonymous *Rare Triumphs of Love and Fortune*, a court play of 1582, Troilus and Cressida appear as the first exemplum of Love's power:

> *Mercury*. Behold, how Troilus and Cressida
>   Cries out on Love, that framed their decay.
> *Vulcan*. That was like the old wife, when her ale would not
>   come
>   Thrust a firebrand in the grout, and scratch'd her bum.
>
> (p. 155)

A reference in Samuel Rowland's *The Letting of Hvmors*

Blood in the Head-Vaine (1600) is couched in a similarly mocking context:

> Be thou the Lady *Cresset-light* to mee,
> Sir Trollelollie I will prooue to thee.   (sig. C₈)

And Marston uses the same pun in the play within *Histriomastix*. Although he starts the play as if it were to be innocently romantic — "*Troylus* was a true lover" and Cressida a "dainty dame" — his actual attitude appears when he has the prologue compare her to the "Christall streame, that runs along ye street." This "home-spun country stuffe" continues:

> *Troy.* Come *Cressida* my Cresset light,
>   Thy face doth shine both day and night,
>   Behold, behold, thy garter blue,
>   Thy knight his valiant elboe weares,
>   That When he shakes his furious Speare,
>   The foe in shivering fearefull sort,
>   May lay him downe in death to snort.
> *Cres.* O knight with vallour in thy face,
>   Here take my skreene weare it for grace,
>   Within thy Helmet put the same,
>   Therewith to make thine enemies lame.   (p. 265)

There is no more of "Troilus and Cressida," and we must agree with Landulpho that it is "Lame stuffe indeed the like was never heard" because it seems manufactured only to be a part of this mocking play.

In spite of these popular and coterie uses of Cressida's name, Shakespeare would not have been blind to Chaucer's and Henryson's gestures of sympathy toward their heroine. To what degree he could have or would have been swayed by these overtures is conjectural, for even in its source as available to Shakespeare Cressida's character is not clearly separate from her sixteenth-century status. On the other hand, the Pandarus of Chaucer is clearly separate from the Elizabethan common noun "pandar"; the gulf was so great by Shakespeare's day that the epithet Sir was necessary to distinguish Chaucer's Pandar from the "pandar" in Paul's yard. Hippolito in *Blurt, Master-Constable* (by Thomas Middleton?) asks Violetta's page if he is "Sir Pandarus, the broking knight of Troy" (II. i. 117). Naturally, Troilus, the true lover, suffered from the company he kept; when Hippolito says that Frenchmen are "as valiant as Troilus" he uses this typical romance phrase in a sexual context (I. i. 143–144). But there was another Troilus, the one of Lydgate and Caxton, who was a bold knight second in prowess only to Hector among the Trojans: as Caxton said, "ther was not in alle the Royame a more strong ne more hardy young man" (II. 543).

It was this Troilus and not the lover that Heywood chose in his *Apology for Actors* (1612) as one of those characters of the public stage who stimulated virtuous action in the spectators. Aristotle, Heywood said, had the destruction of Troy acted before young Alexander for the double purpose of showing the adverse effects of "the lust of Hellena" and "the valor of Achilles." Alexander was so stimulated by what he saw that he conquered the world:

to see a souldier shap'd like a souldier, walke, speake, act like a souldier; to see a Hector all besmered in blood, trampling upon the bulkes of kinges; a Troilus returning from the field, in sight of his father Priam, as if man and horse, even from the steed's rough fetlockes to the plume on the champion's helmet, had bene together plunged into a purple ocean . . . Oh, these were sights to make an Alexander!   (pp. 20–21)

J. S. P. Tatlock was misleading when he said that the medieval accounts of the siege of Troy showed the heroes without any "consciousness of any lofty heroic dignity to be lived up to." [8] The dignity of a blood-besmirched helm and sword was a kind of heroic fulfillment still praiseworthy in Elizabethan England. In Caxton's *Recuyell* it was quite acceptable that Achilles, when he saw Troilus undefended, "ran vpon hym in a rage/ And smote of[f] his heed And caste hit vnder the feet of the horse"; however, when he tied the body to his horse's tail and drew it through the army, the act lacked dignity: "O what vylonnye was hit to drawe so the sone of so noble a kynge / that was so worthy and so hardy / Certes yf ony noblesse had ben in Achilles / he wold not haue done this vylonye" (II. 639).

Caxton occasionally moralized in this manner, but for the most part his long work is an unsophisticated compilation and translation of traditional material. Thus the work retains signs of the original Dictys anti-Trojan attack on the Romans.[9] Because the Dictys manuscript emphasizes that Priam's rash desire to revenge wounded honor, not Venus' prize to Paris, was the motivating cause of the war, Caxton repeated the claim that the award of Helen to Paris could not have been made had Priam not afforded the occasion for Paris' journey. And even in Caxton, in their embassy to Ilium at the beginning of the siege, Ulysses and Diomedes are openly generous, wise, merciful heroes trying to save the rude, headstrong Trojans from unnecessary loss and disaster (II. 556–562). Achilles, whose pagan wrath was termed barbaric by Vergil, in the Dictys story counsels wisely against undertaking the siege, only kills Hector so that the devastating war will not be prolonged, shows his humanity by falling in love with Polyxena, argues against continuing the siege with the clear-sightedness of Shakespeare's Hector, but is killed in a temple through the treachery of Paris. The Trojans are responsible for their own doom, and their worth is strongly questioned. The sons of Priam are even "tote mowthed" and Hector is "A wolf Rauysshying and Insacyable" who lisps (II. 543, 580).

Dares counterattacked in behalf of his Trojan ancestors, but he did not eliminate Dictys' slurs. Both men were presented by their respective anonymous authors as actual participants in the Trojan war who had a mutual revulsion for the *post facto*, hearsay account of the war presented to the world by Homer who had not even been born to witness the events and who was blind at that. As a result, although Dares challenged the claims of Dictys, both men were anti-Homeric and in contrast to Homer's elevated, heroic, heaven-invoking treatment of men and events they tried to capture a realistic, on the spot, confidential picture of things as they actually were. Not only was the Greek of Homer lost to the Middle Ages, but being a Greek "naturally" he had lied, and since Dictys was openly pro-Greek, the Middle Ages embraced the crude Latin account of Dares as gospel. In good medieval manner each succeeding redactor of the matter of Troy acknowledged Dares as his authority (ignoring, of course, his immediate sources and wonderfully oblivious of the chronological questions surrounding the Dictys and Dares manuscripts). Even Sidney claims in the *Defence* that the true account of Aeneas, an ancient fifth-columnist, is not to be found in Vergil the poet but in Dares the historian. Thus Caxton's *Recuyell*, which Douglas Bush believes "far more than any other book . . . established the Elizabethan conception of the Trojan war," [10] is a compilation of all the various attitudes toward and accounts of the fall of Troy: "Vlixes was the moste fayr man among all the grekes / *But was deceyuable And subtyll*. And sayd his thynges Ioyously. *He was a right grete lyar* And was so well bespoken that he had none felawe ne like to hym" (II. 541). The italics are mine and show how in its latest and most expanded form Dares' detraction of Ulysses is interspersed casually with Dictys' praise. Furthermore, Caxton's text contains an interesting pair of attributions: according to Dictys,

Ajax was a more important warrior than Achilles, but to Dares he was a mad fool.

Thus, even though Benoît and his followers added the medieval trappings of expanded truces and knightly oaths and jousts (which by their very nature tended to turn the public dignity of Dictys' Achilles into selfish pride) and in spite of the general European pro-Trojan bias, an underlying ambivalence persisted in the matter of Troy right down to Shakespeare's day. For this reason, as Harry Levin suggests, the name of Priam was "as much a byword for catastrophe to the Elizabethans as the name Hiroshima seems to us"; [11] yet his son Hector was an emblem of the ideal scholarly, soldierly, and honest man in spite of his key position in Ilium.

This inherent ambivalence would not be apparent necessarily to anyone reading the matter of Troy for its action or story alone, nor is it sufficiently strong to prevent anyone's retaining a preconceived pro-Trojan bias after having read the story. But if anyone attempted to read the material with an eye to characterization the story might begin to appear at least quaint if not ridiculous; if one happened to look for meaning he would be forced to find it illustrated mainly through negative example.

George Peele's *The Tale of Troy* (1589) is an important analogue to Shakespeare's play because it reflects Elizabethan rather than medieval tones and attitudes. Although the poem shows the experimental influence of Spenser in its style, its content is strictly traditional: it is, in fact, a five-hundred-line epitome of Book III of Caxton's chronicle. For this reason it is interesting to note that the poem opens in an uncritical pro-Trojan manner, but is soon critical of Paris' having been swayed by mere exterior beauty. This moral tone, however, is dropped completely during an amused, "witty" description of his wooing of Helen. Still, when

Helen is about to leave for Troy the tone becomes serious again, but in a personal, inner way. Although Helen lost her "regard of honour" by succumbing to Paris, she did not become entirely abandoned:

> [When] her hart was from her body hent,
> To Troy this Helen with her Lover went.
> Thinking perdie a part contrary kinde
> Her hart so wrought, her selfe to stay behind.   (ll. 173–178)

The tone continues to change as various attitudes are expressed. The honor of each side is equally stressed, yet the Greeks are dismissed as subtle traitors and the Trojans are accused of "ryot, rape and vaine credulitie" (l. 410). Hector and Achilles are described as wild animals, but in an obviously positive, heroic context (ll. 302–325). Chivalry is praised for making men "bold and venturous" (l. 278); elsewhere, policy is called "The sinews and true strength of Chivalrie" (l. 361). The ten years' siege is progressively a "quarrell" (l. 199), a "tragicke sport" (l. 258), and a "wastfull warre" (l. 374). And in a familiar contrast Troilus is stimulated to noble action "all for pure love of the unconstant Cressid" (l. 280), who is unworthy of a full description. Although he dismisses her as a mere "chaunging peece" (l. 283), Peele is not so hard on Helen; he even attempts to speak "in favour of her name" in an epilogue (ll. 486–493).

This situation is reversed within Robert Greene's handling of the Troy material in *Euphues, His Censure to Philautus* (1587). Because he used the legend as a frame for various romantic tales, the actual story was secondary in Greene's treatment. He shows the main rivals of the Trojan War in a period of truce holding conversations which focus on certain general moral issues concerning the nature of the true warrior. The various qualities which are suggested as necessary are then illustrated by the tales. Thus we are afforded an opportunity of seeing how one

Elizabethan extracted characterization and thematic issues from the Troy material.

Whereas Peele was gentle with Helen, Greene was with Cressida. Although in one of the tales reference is made to her proverbial unchaste nature, in the frame sequence she is merely a Greek lady who helps to entertain the visiting Trojan knights and ladies. In fact she is rather a bluestocking, taunting Hector — in language quite similar to that which Shakespeare gives his own Hector — about the Trojans' wasting blood in defense of a worthless woman all because of honor. Hector evades the issue by saying that the Trojans fight not on grounds of honor, "but as holding it princely, with death to requite an iniury" (pp. 166–167). But Euphues tells us that Helen was a scourge for the sin and folly of Troy; the nation fell because the Trojans sowed the seeds of their own destruction when they were led by "voluptuos appetites" to honor Helen "more for her beawty then hir honesty (a fault which fondlings account for a fauour)" (pp. 155–156). Although this same kind of reasoning in the play lies behind Ulysses' pondering why fancy leads men to value external beauty over inner virtue, the oratorical styles of Euphues and Ulysses reveal utterly different characterizations.

Greene's Troilus is quite similar to Shakespeare's. When the Greeks (who like Shakespeare's Troilus and Paris have been educated on the works of Plato and Aristotle) get the better of the debate on moral qualities (p. 199), Troilus asks haughtily if the enemy wants to fight by philosophy or by the sword. Then after a tale which illustrates that *sapiens* must come before *fortis*, Troilus shouts indignantly that such a claim is nonsense; but Nestor quietly replies that "without wisedome hee [the warrior] shall fall eyther to excesse or defect: eyther to bee too fearefull, or too rashe" (p. 232).

Because the scenes all take place during the banqueting of

knights and their ladies, the frame of *Euphues*, like Chaucer's *Troilus*, has a strong aura of romance. However, a certain sense of sterility is felt in Greene's work because the medieval background of knightly action has been replaced by talk, and the courtly, superficial effect of much of this talk is reinforced by the fashionable wit which is displayed by Euphues as he manipulates the frame. It is not surprising that a few critics have felt that a consciously satiric, ethical analysis of the Trojan war was part of Greene's purpose, and that *Euphues, His Censure to Philautus* might have been a guiding stimulus to Shakespeare.

One, C. H. Herford, after remarking how the courtly byplay in Greene's *Euphues* reflects the continuance of a medieval tradition with regard to Troy even in an age regarded now as an era of return to the classics, goes on to observe that of course even Chapman "only half broke with the tradition." [12] Chapman's expansion of Hector's character gave the epic two heroes, and his ethical bias turned the amoral original into an Elizabethan book of conduct for courtiers.[13] Robert K. Presson suggests that Shakespeare may have turned to Chapman's Homer in search of a fresh approach to a story with obvious contemporary commercial value, and his full and detailed study of Shakespeare's probable sources reveals how much of Chapman's translation could have been useful to Shakespeare in plotting the siege story. Although Presson feels that "the dramatist's debt to the incomplete 1598 edition of Homer is manifest . . . in the central situation, in the episodes, in narrative flavor, theme or conception, and in characterization," [14] we should recall that Chapman's elevation of Homer did not displace the medieval Troy legend or erase the medieval distrust of the ancient, pagan poet. Heywood noted in his *Troia Britanica* (1609) that he really did not know whether Homer or Dares was correct about the reason for Achilles'

withdrawal, but in his *Iron Age* (1609) he did not hesitate
to attribute Achilles' refusal to fight to his love of Polyxena.
In *An Apology for Actors* (1612), he called Achilles a dramatic example of "magnanimity," but in the *Iron Age* he
showed Achilles playing the part of a bully.

In showing an inconsistent attitude toward Achilles, Heywood was consistent with his age. Long before Chapman,
Sidney had been full of praise for Homer and his Greek
hero; yet Anthony Gibson printed a reaction to the *Iliad*
in 1599 which runs counter to both Sidney and Chapman.
In his *A Womans Worth*, written in praise of women and
dedicated with fashionable flourish to the Queen and the
ladies of her court, we are told that the "*Illiades* [is] a worke
in sooth praise worthy," but only because Homer was literate
in an age of barbarism and "not for any other consideration."
One wonders what Gibson might have thought of Chapman's recent translation, since he found Homer atheistical,
immodest, barbaric, and contemptible. The *Iliad* is dangerous reading because Homer established "a contempt of
royalty, duty, and obeyance, in the person of Achillis (a
meere brothell hunter) who preferred a bruitish kinde of
affection [for the slave girl Briseis], before the loue of his
Country, and his owne peculiar hate, before the general
welfare of his followers." Gibson was not motivated by an
attempt to propagandize the side of the Trojans; their hero,
Hector, as portrayed by Homer, is a mere "mad man" (pp.
16–17). This sampling of late Elizabethan ethical opinions
shows that Shakespeare could have used Homer, even Chapman's Homer, but that he would not have been obligated
to follow any one, established attitude toward the *Iliad*.

Ever since Dr. Johnson, certain scholars have felt that
Shakespeare must have used Homer if only because of his
satiric observer of the human scene, Thersites. But Thersites
can be cited in support of the claim that Shakespeare's

knowledge of Homer may have been indirect only, for his study of rhetoric certainly introduced him to the main persons and attitudes which are presented in the *Iliad*. Although Thersites appears but briefly in Homer, his deformed appearance and rude behavior were sufficiently vivid that he was given a secure place in Latin rhetoric books as an example of the railing detractor.[15] Thus his name had a means of continuous currency as a rhetorical type while the *Iliad* was forgotten during the Middle Ages, and he descended to the Elizabethans with no necessary dependence on Homer, as can be seen in Leonard Cox's *The Arte or Crafte of Rhethoryke*. Before describing the rhetorical mode which Thersites illustrates, Cox briefly reviews his role in the *Iliad*; he then goes on to say that Thersites provides an example of detraction because he was "ryght foule mouthed / and ful of debate and stryfe / carrynge alwayes agaynst the heddes and wyse men of the armye" (p. 53).

The interlude *Thersites* (c. 1562) is a full, but rather innocuous dramatization of Thersites' rhetorical function as it had been illustrated by Johannes Revisius Textor in a pedagogical Latin verse dialogue. Yet in Textor and the English imitation Thersites was assumed to be so well known that he is placed in a setting that is outside the *Iliad*. When he first appears, he tells us that he had just returned from "the Siege of Troy" and says,

In Homer of my acts ye have read, I trow:
Neither Agamemnon nor Ulysses I spared to check, (p. 395)

but the interlude is mainly an extended illustration of Thersites' railing — for example, against motherhood and Christianity — and is built to a climax that reveals him as a complete coward.

Heywood also illustrated the role of Thersites in one of his *Pleasant Dialogues and Drammas*. Furthermore, he tells us in a note that Thersites appeared in the *Iliad* "as crooked in minde as in body," and that he has been so famous that the proverb "*Thersite faedior*" arose and "hath continued even to this day" (p. 242). When in 1591, Thomas Bradshaw says in *The Sheperd's Starre* that "in a prouerbe they call it *Thersitica facies*" whenever ugliness is found in an ill-mannered person (sig. E₂v), because his proverb differs from Heywood's, we can see again how independent Thersites was of Homer and that an Elizabethan audience would have recognized him as a walking, talking figure of speech.

We are not reduced to searching through text books and proverbs, however, in order to account for Thersites; rather, his characterization is another example of how pervasive was the "matter of Troy" in Shakespeare's day. I have intentionally touched upon some of the lesser known aspects of its heritage, aspects which Shakespeare himself may not have realized. Yet it should never be forgotten how broad and thorough was Shakespeare's exposure to and knowledge of the Trojan war. In school he must have had to frame many a debate on moral and ethical questions abstracted from situations that occurred in the siege of Troy; [16] out of school he must have spent many hours over Lydgate, Prince Hal's poet and Chaucer's compeer in the sixteenth century.[17] And finally it would be almost impossible to overemphasize the great influence of Vergil and Ovid not merely on an Elizabethan schoolboy but more importantly on an Elizabethan poet.

THE "MATTER OF TROY" IN THE CANON

Because Shakespeare's education was, to use our term, classical, allusions to the matter of Troy abound in the canon, but their number increased markedly in the years before *Troilus and Cressida*. Although Tatlock believed that this increase shows Shakespeare's awareness of the current commercial exploitation of the material, in print and on the stage, Kittredge felt that it reflects Shakespeare's growing personal interest in the story of Troy.[18] Regardless of who was right, and both well may have been, a survey of these allusions will help prepare the way for a reading of the play that Shakespeare ultimately made of the matter of Troy.

The only truely sympathetic reference in the canon to Troilus and Cressida comes in the last scene of *The Merchant of Venice* when, in order to set the mood and establish the time, Shakespeare has Lorenzo and Jessica try to outwit each other in recalling traditional lovesick characters in various night settings; Lorenzo opens by saying that

> in such a night
> Troilus methinks mounted the Troyan walls
> And sigh'd his soul toward the Grecian tents,
> Where Cressid lay that night.   (V. i. 3–6)

Other references are not so gentle. After having received one coin from Viola in disguise, Feste in *Twelfth Night* attempts to get another by saying, "I would play Lord Pandarus of Phrygia, sir, to bring a Cressida to this Troilus" so that they may breed. When she applauds and rewards his clever begging, he replies, "The matter, I hope, is not great, sir, begging but a beggar: Cressida was a beggar" (III. i. 54–61). Whereas Lorenzo refers to the story of Troilus and Cressida as told by Chaucer, Feste knows the story as it was completed by Henryson, and it was in this total context that the story was known in Shakespeare's day. Shakespeare reproduces a popular image when he has Pistol in *Henry V* call Doll Tearsheet a "lazar kite of Cressid's kind" (II. i. 80).

Shakespeare based his presentation of Troilus in great measure upon his proverbial faithfulness, but faced with Cressida's nature, he found that he had to mute this abstract quality at the end of the play lest Troilus appear ridiculous. References to Troilus in the canon show how exacting

Shakespeare's problem was, for they reflect the necessary vacuity of someone who insisted on being faithful to a false woman. In *The Taming of the Shrew*, Petruchio calls his spaniel "Troilus" (IV. i. 153). In *Much Ado about Nothing*, Benedick, bemoaning his inability to pen verse after he has fallen in love, says that "Leander the good swimmer, Troilus the first employer of panders, and a whole book full of these quondam carpet-mongers, whose names yet run smoothly in the even road of a blank verse — why, they were never so truly turn'd over and over as my poor self in love" (V. ii. 30–36). And in *As You Like It*, Rosalind, disguised as Ganymede and pretending to be Rosalind, ridicules Orlando when he says that he will die if his beloved should reject him: "Troilus had his brains dash'd out with a Grecian club; yet he did what he could to die before, and he is one of the patterns of love . . . Men have died from time to time, and worms have eaten them, but not for love" (IV. i. 96–108). Although these references are all in a light vein, they are in perfect decorum from the point of view of each speaker. The inference is that the material selected for the speaker is likewise in perfect decorum.

Strange as it may seem at first, the pathetic description which Shakespeare gives of the siege of Troy in *Lucrece* is also in perfect decorum. There he shows Lucrece sublimating the personal grief brought on through Tarquin's lust by recalling the general grief of her ancestors; however, Shakespeare did not have to distort the legend of Troy to fit this special purpose. Paris' lust for Helen, in tradition as in the painting, was the cause of the fall of Troy. Accessories to the crime are Helen, "the strumpet that began this stir" (ll. 1471), and "credulous, old Priam":

> Had doting Priam check'd his son's desire,
> Troy had been bright with fame, and not with fire.

.   .   .   .

Priam, why art thou old, and yet not wise?

>   (ll. 1490–1491, 1550)

In *Troilus and Cressida* there is a possible implication that
Priam is not wise; in light of this reference perhaps drawing
such an inference is sound.

While Ajax is presented simply as a warrior in *Lucrece*,
Ulysses is presented with the ambivalence found in Caxton:

> In Ajax's eyes blunt rage and rigour roll'd;
>   But the mild glance that sly Ulysses lent
>   Show'd deep regard and smiling government.
>
>   (ll. 1398–1400)

Ajax and Ulysses are paired because of their traditional contention for the armor of Achilles. Because Sophocles and
Ovid emphasized that Ajax became insane when the armor
was awarded to Ulysses, there arose the derivative tradition
reinforced by Dares which turned Ajax into a kind of mad
fool. Thus in *Love's Labour's Lost*, Berowne can say that
"love is as mad as Ajax" (IV. iii. 7); yet in the same play
Ajax the warrior is mentioned, as usual, in pun, along with
the worthies of antiquity (V. ii. 581). Although Achilles
appears only briefly in *Lucrece*, he is a warrior respected
for his prowess. And, although Agamemnon is not mentioned by name, he is surely one of the commanders whose

>   grace and majesty
> You might behold triumphing in their faces. (ll. 1388–1389)

Even in a Roman painting described by a British descendent
of the Trojans, there is no anti-Greek bias.

Shakespeare had no need to reflect a prejudice in *Lucrece*,
for the fall of Troy was accepted as historical fact. As such,
it was material from which moral lessons could be drawn.
For example, Hector, here and throughout the early plays,

is called the hope of Troy because of his brave leadership even though his leadership was in an ill-fated cause. Both he and Troilus die because of Paris's passion for Helen: "one man's lust these many lives confounds" (l. 1489). And the strain on Hecuba of a weak-minded husband and passionate son made her the epitome of "Time's ruin, beauty's wrack, and grim care's reign" (l. 1451). This treatment of the fall of Troy, as generally in the early plays, echoes the respectful pathos of Vergil's version in the *Aeneid*. Thus the atmosphere of high seriousness in the painting is both accurate and appropriate to Lucrece's predicament, just as the legend provided Marcus Andronicus with an appropriate simile with which to introduce his nephew Lucius at the close of *Titus Andronicus*:

> Speak, Rome's dear friend, as erst our ancestor,
> When with his solemn tongue he did discourse
> To lovesick Dido's sad-attending ear
> The story of that baleful-burning night
> When subtile Greeks surpris'd King Priam's Troy.
>
> (V. iii. 80–84)

But the material of Troy was hardly sacrosanct. Hector as one of the worthies in Holofernes' pageant at the end of *Love's Labour's Lost* is ridiculed by the nobles in order that they may upset Armado in his acting. Still, Armado's retort is touching: "The sweet war-man is dead and rotten. Sweet chucks, beat not the bones of the buried: when he breathed, he was a man" (V. ii. 666–668). The host in *The Merry Wives of Windsor* calls Falstaff, "bully Hector" (I. iii. 11) and Doctor Caius, "Hector of Greece" (II. iii. 35). Doll Tearsheet tells Falstaff in *2 Henry IV* that he is "as valorous as Hector of Troy, worth five of Agamemnon, and ten times better than the Nine Worthies" (II. iv. 236–239). And we have already noted how Pistol, that "fustian rascal" who constantly apes the bombast of plays, has tags from the Troy legend ready on his lips.

When he calls Falstaff's Doll in 2 *Henry IV* the "Helen of thy noble thoughts" (V. v. 35) he is probably unaware of any comic irony. The "strumpet" she was called in *Lucrece* was indeed her status in the public eye. According to the author of *The Lamentation of Troy for the Death of Hector* (1594), "Helen the whore wrought *Troys* decay" (l. 1054). Thus, Orlando, writing in praise of Rosalind in *As You Like It*, says that she has "Helen's cheek, but not her heart" (III. ii. 153); the distinction was all important if he did not wish to alienate his beloved. And the clown in *All's Well*, who in the opinion of Peter Seng is "addicted . . . to scurrilous rhymes," [19] sings a song which begins:

> "Was this fair face the cause," quoth she,
>   "Why the Grecians sacked Troy?
> Fond done, done fond!
>   Was this King Priam's joy?"   (I. iii. 74–77)

The tone here is unmistakable, but no one seems to have caught entirely the spirit of the "player's speech" in *Hamlet*.[20]

If Shakespeare had satire or parody as a secondary intention in writing the lines for the player, he did not allow that intention to destroy the primary dramatic purpose of the speech. All would agree that it is "a passionate speech," that it is consciously differentiated from the style of the play proper, and that it is about a person opposite in nature to Hamlet himself. That it is from "Aeneas' tale to Dido" and that an educated Hamlet likes and is moved by it seem sufficiently strong evidence that the speech as a whole is intended to be taken seriously within the context of the play. Even though certain words and phrases in the player's lines and the entire episode out of context do suggest some ulterior

motive, that motive does not reveal any attitude toward the
material of Troy either more or less serious than previously
noted. Shakespeare does not here adopt the mocking view
of his material which he displays in the play of "Pyramus
and Thisby" in *A Midsummer Night's Dream* or the satiric
view of his material which he displays in *Venus and Adonis*.
Although there is a difference between myth and history,
these examples of parody and satire should remind us that
it is illogical to expect Shakespeare to assume a modern
romantic, somewhat stylized approach to the traditional
materials of Western culture. Because they were not antique
but real to him, he paid them the tribute of free and unconscious artistic adaptation.

We saw at the beginning of this chapter that a play on
Troy may have been economically feasible about 1601. That
Shakespeare's use of the Troy legend increased as the canon
approached *Troilus* may reflect the popularity of the material, as Tatlock believed, or it may only show Shakespeare's
personal interest in it, as Kittredge believed. In either case
these references are inconclusive as evidence of a narrowly
defined Shakespearean attitude toward the matter of Troy;
indeed, his use of the story and its characters reflects in
miniature the wide variety, contradictions, and stereotypes
prevalent in the Trojan literary tradition. The references in
other plays reflect the same variety, although the coterie
plays reflect a rather superior, less moralizing attitude toward
this perennially popular fare. In general, whatever attitude
Shakespeare may have wished to assume in *Troilus*, the story
and its literary, traditional, and theatrical heritage afforded
God's plenty from which he could choose. If in 1601 he decided or was asked to attempt a coterie approach to the
writing of a public play, the Troy material could have suggested itself because of its established public drawing power,

while at the same time it was particularly suited for experimenting with the new vein of drama which seemed to be concerned more with lust than with love, with attitudes than with action, with clever and stupid schemes than with valiant or villainous deeds, and with satiric humor than with romantic laughter.[21]

CHAPTER IV · THE PLOT OF THE PLAY
AND THE PROBLEM OF STRUCTURE

*I*N DEFENDING the artistic merits of the drama against the claims of *belles lettres* and pictorial art Thomas Heywood remarked in the *Apology for Actors* that "A description is only a shadow, received by the eare, but not perceived by the eye; [and] lively portrature is meerely a forme seene by the eye, but can neither shew action, passion, motion, or any other gesture to moove the spirits of the beholder to admiration" (p. 20). What seemed significant to Heywood is that drama is a complex of diverse elements and appeals: a play is a planned combination of action and speech, presented through characters, which tells a story to an audience. Drama is, then, in its end, simple, its prime purpose being to tell a story, or, to use Shakespeare's favorite phrase, "to please." And though it does so through the interweaving of actions, characters, themes, and the resources of language, to tell a story effectively a play must be firmly framed within the author's conception and projection of a story-line. Plot is the *sine qua non* of drama not because Aristotle said so; rather, as Aristotle's analysis of many plays revealed, plot is essential because it creates the logic of a play's action, controls the environment of its characters, and shapes the statement of its themes. The plot leads all the dramatic elements into the final image which evolves from a play; if it is not well managed, the final image will be blurred.

Because analysis by nature is abstract and prose by nature, flattening, no critic can ever describe fully the final dramatic image of a play — that would necessitate the presentation of the play itself. But criticism and art are separate matters. Although specialized disciplines and particular schools can shed light on various historical and aesthetic aspects of a play, the most any critic of the printed drama ultimately can hope to do is to help a reader to respond to a text as if it were being presented before him, letting it fill the vistas of the mind.

With these simple generic assumptions and critical principles in mind I wish to show in this chapter how Shakespeare shaped the matter of Troy into a plot for *Troilus and Cressida*, how he designed the play to unfold before an audience. The play so "seen" raises an immediate question: is this sound dramaturgy? But other questions also arise. Why is there such a diversity of action, character, and language? What kind of people are in the play? How are we to respond to its major concerns? In seeking to lay the foundations for answers to such questions I focus here on the question of the structural effectiveness of the plot of *Troilus and Cressida*, but in so doing I hope to suggest that each of the three plot-lines is itself a major critical area requiring further analysis and study. The method here will also be that of the three succeeding chapters. After trying to isolate through analysis a critical "problem" I shall turn both to the canon and to the competing repertories in order to find those touches in and aspects of other plays which may help us to understand the puzzling parts and strange effects — "the problems" — of *Troilus and Cressida*.

To suggest that it may be profitable to look in Shakespeare's plays before *Troilus and Cressida* for signs and tokens of things to come, is not to imply that his work is of whole cloth, progressively more subtly and expertly woven. Because there are several kinds of drama and an infinite number of stories to be told, no two plays can be compared without being contrasted, and not merely contrasted qualitatively. Even the plays of a single writer will be different one from another: *Edward II* and *The Jew of Malta* have as little in common as *Richard II* and *The Merchant of Venice*. Nevertheless, since the present concern is how Shakespeare executed the story of *Troilus and Cressida*, a review of the canon that attempts neither to be rigorously chronological, nor to include full analyses of single plays, can be helpful in showing us Shakespeare's usual techniques and developing structural procedures. And because the theatrical setting of *Troilus* is a dynamic one a comparison and contrast of the plot of this play with the plots of competing plays should give us an answer to the problem of structure.

THE BASIC STRUCTURE AND BEGINNING ACTION

Troilus and Cressida has three main locales, each of which is associated with a main plot-line and has its own thematic environment because of the kind of action which takes place within it. Pandarus' House — which with Elizabethan casualness is also called Cressida's as well as Calchas' — introduces the love plot which mainly touches on the motif of love and lust; Priam's Palace, or "Ilium," introduces the Trojan plot-line which mainly analyzes the demands of honor and war on the individual; and the Greek Camp introduces a plot-line which mainly explores the implications of order and disorder in man and society. The action moves through each of these locales until the three plot-lines are finally brought together and resolved in a fourth locale, the Battlefield.

The actual design of the plot within this general pattern of movement is more complicated and carefully considered; for example, Aeneas early visits the Greek camp, Troilus joins the council at Ilium, Diomedes visits both Ilium and Pandarus' house, and most scenes in given locales are framed with references to the other locales. As a result the thematic motifs are developed not in strict isolation, but in mutual support of each other; and the action does not suddenly come from three isolated areas to be resolved in the final battle, but is gradually funneled toward the field by a narrowing of the over-all plot.

As in any play, the basic beginning action, middle action, and final action are rather easily discerned. One does not feel, however, breaking or turning points, for the action is continuous throughout. After the plot-elements all have been introduced in five scenes, they are developed and complicated in the next eleven, and are resolved in the last eight. There are no act-divisions, although editors usually supply the traditional four and T. W. Baldwin has made a structural analysis of the play based upon this division into five acts.[1] Although the plot of *Troilus* unifies the action, it does not embrace a logical report of time and pays only the most general attention to place: the day that falls before the Hector-Ajax trial by arms is described severally as a day of war and a day of truce, and the trial occurs in the battlefield without the stage's having been cleared of what has been established as a scene in the Greek camp. Such disregard of the unities would not be found in a play which followed the academic formula for the five-act structure. But this conjectural rebuttal is hardly necessary. Convincing empirical evidence cannot be deduced in support of five acts for *Troilus and Cressida*. Although there are not really twenty-four scenes in the play, reference throughout is to the traditional act-scene division so that the analysis may be followed in any standard text.

The beginning action gives one the impression that it has three scenes each of which introduces a main locale, the characters, and the thematic motifs of one of the plot-lines. First, a senile and titillated Pandarus works to bring together an infatuated, passionate Troilus and a willing, but calculating Cressida (I. i + ii). Then, a wise but close-dealing Ulysses tries to repair the chain of command in the

Greek camp, his method being at first an oblique suggestion couched in the high-powered philosophical disquisition on "Order" that Agamemnon assert himself (I. iii), but then he shifts after Hector's challenge has been delivered by Aeneas to a ruse both patriotic and subversive: he will shame Achilles out of his retirement from battle because of his love for Polyxena by having the blockish Ajax announced as the best man to answer the challenge (I. iii + II. i). And, finally, in a parallel council scene Hector, backed by Helenus, intelligently, objectively, and idealistically debates with Troilus, backed by Paris, the question of the validity of a war waged over a woman stolen from her husband and remaining the willing mistress of her enemy; yet Hector sophistically, subjectively, and realistically understands the futility of trying to change the course of a state committed to a policy of seven long years. In fact, Hector further undercuts the effect of his initial position when he announces that even before the debate he had challenged any Greek to defend the reputation of this lady in a trial by combat, an act alone which would force this war of "honor" to continue (II. ii). All the talk takes the plot nowhere.

THE MIDDLE ACTION

Hector's challenge, however, appears as if it will be used to draw the plot-lines together into a climax within the middle action. While the Greeks prepare Ajax to meet the challenge (II. iii), Paris and Helen show their essential lack of concern about all matters including the challenge (III. i.), and Troilus and Cressida are brought together by Pandarus in an affair about which Troilus seems more inclined to talk and Cressida to be indifferent (III. ii). Thersites opens II. iii railing in monologue against his betters, but inadvertently characterizes himself as well: "How now, Thersites? What, lost in the labyrinth of thy fury? Shall the elephant Ajax

carry it thus? He beats me, and I rail at him. O worthy
satisfaction! Would it were otherwise: that I could beat him
whilst he rail'd at me. 'Sfoot, I'll learn to conjure and raise
devils but I'll see some issue of my spiteful execrations"
(1–8). He lacks purpose, is malcontent, and curses loudly
and evilly only out of spite. After he denounces both Ajax
and Achilles for their "little little less than little wit," Patroclus enters and draws his attention. When Achilles finally
enters we then get an example of the kind of fatuous mim-
icry which Ulysses has said seems so to delight Achilles of
late. But this mocking of the chain of command is interrupted by the arrival of Agamemnon and his counsellors before it establishes any point. Achilles withdraws, taking with
him Thersites, whose parting words summarize his view of
the story of the play: "All the argument is a whore and a
cuckold — a good quarrel to draw emulous factions and
bleed to death upon. Now, the dry suppeago on the subject,
and war and lechery confound all!" (78–82). And the scene
continues with a series of ineffectual attempts to get Achilles
to confer with Agememnon interspersed with open baiting
and ridicule of Ajax.

The scene in Paris' apartment (III. i) is mildly humorous,
but in the way that Restoration comedy later will be humorous: fashionable people meet in a sitting room and talk
cleverly and smartly about nothing. If one is charmed by
the sophistication of late seventeenth-century comedy, then
he might agree with Alice Walker that this is "the most brilliant scene of pure comedy in the canon"; [2] if not, then, as
it seems to L. C. Knights and H. N. Hillebrand, this "silly
smart-talk" is apt to appear to be "trivial chatter in a moral
vacuum." [3] F. W. Sternfeld endorses this second opinion in
his excellent study of the use of music in the play, and especially in this scene, concluding that Pandarus' "courtly, sophisticated, self-indulgent lecherous song ["Love, love,

nothing but love"] characterizes the ills with which the
Trojan gentry is infested." [4] When Helen says, "this love will
undo us all" and Paris, in contrast to Hector later, confesses,
"I would fain have arm'd today, but my Nell would not
have it so," the lines help establish directly what the whole
scene connotes: a kind of lethargy, a feeling of emptiness,
permeates Ilium. And the conclusion emphasizes that this
environment is not separate from that of the previous council scene at the palace, for at the end an alarm sounds to
remind us that the war is being fought so that scenes like
this may go on. Paris suggests that they go to "Priam's hall/
To greet the warriors" and, when Helen agrees, Paris mumbles in adoration, "Sweet, above thought I love thee!" Such
also will be Antony's decision, but at least his has a touch
of the sublime in it. The effect of the scene is such that we
nod in bewildered agreement with F. P. Wilson, "Was *this*
the face that launched a thousand ships"? [5]

In this scene Pandarus had tried to lay a smoke screen behind which Troilus could meet Cressida. His effort was
useless; everyone knew what was about to take place. In fact
Pandarus all but gave the plan away because of his obvious
titillation. Hence, having him act as he did and with whom
he did establishes in advance a quality of illicitness and pru-
rience for the assignation scene (III. ii) which follows. After
much delay Pandarus is able to bring together a passionate,
naïve Troilus and a calculating, world-weary Cressida. [6] The
way that they pledge their love demonstrates how well the
audience knew the story of the lovers because the ironic
mode of presentation rests on the assumption that everyone
believed that Troilus was going to be true, that Cressida was
going to be false, and that "Pandar" was another name for
a procurer. At the end of the scene this sense of detachment
from the characters is increased when all three join hands in
a sense of unity and security:

Pandarus. Go to, a bargain made! Seal it, seal it; I'll be the witness . . . If ever you prove false one to another . . . Let all constant men be Troiluses, all false women Cressids, and all brokers-between Pandars! Say, "Amen."   (III. ii. 204–212)

With each separate "Amen," so confidently repeated three times, the characters are placed at further removes from the audience that knows full well what the outcome of their story will be. And this feeling of alienation is capped by Pandarus' closing, obscene blessings, first on the couple and then on the women in the audience. A scene which began with Troilus' hurried expectation ends in talk; interest has been moved from deeds to words.

In each of these three scenes of the middle action each plot-line develops in such a way that it implies its own evaluation or special theme, but with III. iii, the three lines begin to come together. At the opening of the play Pandarus casually mentions that Cressida's father, Calchas, is in the Greek camp and that she ought to follow. Now that event takes shape, as Calchas asks for "my Cressid in right great exchange" for Antenor, who has been captured. Agamemnon agrees and sets in motion the means of involving Cressida in the Greek story at the same time that the structural means by which the Ilium story comes into the Greek camp is reactivated:

> Good Diomed,
> Furnish you fairly for this interchange.
> Withal bring word if Hector will to-morrow
> Be answered in his challenge. Ajax is ready.   (III. iii. 32–35)

After Ulysses movingly warns Achilles that time may pass him by if he remains inactive, and Thersites bitterly castigates the behavior of all the Greeks, in four scenes so short and blended that they give the impression of one, the ex-

change of Antenor and the parting of the lovers take place
(IV. i, ii, iii, + iv).

The parting, even without the complication of the exchange, was not progressing on an even and smooth plane;
now in IV. iv Cressida's opening speech with its self-centered
relish makes the perfect epilogue to the love affair for which
Troilus' "expectation whirls me round" (III. ii. 19) served
as prologue:

> The grief is fine, full, perfect, that I taste,
> And violenteth in a sense as strong
> As that which causeth it. How can I moderate it?
> If I could temporize with my affection
> Or brew it to a weak and colder palate,
> The like allayment could I give my grief.
> My love admits no qualifying dross;
> No more my grief in such a precious loss.   (IV. iv. 3–10)

Pandarus has been and continues to be entertained by the
whole affair; in fact his emotions are so detached from the
present action that he lapses into a short, comic interlude:

> What a pair of spectacles is here! Let me embrace too. "O heart,"
> as the goodly saying is,
>> "O heart, heavy heart,
>> Why sigh'st thou without breaking?"
> where he answers again,
>> "Because thou canst not ease thy smart
>> By friendship nor by speaking."
> There was never a truer rhyme. Let us cast away nothing, for
> we may live to have need of such a verse. We see it, we see it.
> How now, lambs?   (IV. iv. 14–25)

Here, as at his dismissal at the end of the love affair, tags
of song protect Pandarus from facing the full implications
of his actions.

While Pandarus' skit has been going on, there has been

some sort of stage business between the lovers. Troilus now speaks in a conventional trope:

> Cressid, I love thee in so strain'd a purity,
> That the blest gods, as angry with my fancy,
> More bright in zeal than the devotion which
> Cold lips blow to their deities, take thee from me.
>
> (IV. iv. 26–29)

Although one expects either the silence of tears or an effusive outburst from lovers being torn apart, Troilus speaks with a resigned calm. There is sincere regret in his voice, but it is not unmixed with a feeling of fatigue and, almost, a sense of relief:

> Injurious Time now with a robber's haste
> Crams his rich thiev'ry up, he knows not how.
>
> (IV. iv. 44–45)

Aeneas calls, the last words are being exchanged, but peace is beyond the understanding of these lovers:

> *Troilus.* Hear me, my love. Be thou but true of heart —
> *Cressida.* I true? How now! What wicked deem is this?
>
> (IV. iv. 60–61)

Troilus' answer betrays a rather dull mind, but reveals a love of rhetoric:

> I speak not "Be thou true" as fearing thee,
> For I will throw my glove to Death himself
> That there's no maculation in thy heart;
> But "Be thou true" say I to fashion in
> My sequent protestation: Be thou true,
> And I will see thee.   (IV. iv. 64–69)

A self-satisfied smile almost seems to break through. The conversation goes on, Troilus talking too much, and Cressida protesting too much. Somehow they exchange tokens

—a sleeve and a glove—Aeneas and Paris call, and Troilus finally is ready to go: "Come, kiss; and let us part." Now it is Cressida's turn to ask, "My lord, will you be true?" In the place of a plain and simple affirmative we are given a balanced, polished statement to denote plainness and simplicity:

> Who? I? Alas, it is my vice, my fault!
> Whiles others fish with craft for great opinion,
> I with great truth catch mere simplicity.
> Whilst some with cunning gild their copper crowns,
> With truth and plainness I do wear mine bare.
> Fear not my truth. The moral of my wit
> Is "plain and true"; there's all the reach of it.
>
> (IV. iv. 104–110)

Paris, Aeneas, Diomedes, and the rest enter, and Troilus turns without pause to welcome the enemy and to entreat fair usage for Cressida. Diomedes ignores him and speaks to Cressida directly; whereupon Troilus becomes enraged, not so much because of any slight to Cressida but to himself. Diomedes smilingly retorts, "O, be not mov'd, Prince Troilus." Taking the measure of Cressida, he continues in pun and irony:

> When I am hence,
> I'll answer to my lust . . .
> To her own worth
> She shall be priz'd.   (IV. iv. 133–136)

Diomedes, were he a son of Priam, would never have opposed Hector in council. As they all go out, a trumpet sounds, attention is turned again to Hector's challenge, and Aeneas closes the scene on an appropriately heroic note:

> Let us address to tend on Hector's heels.
> The glory of our Troy doth this day lie
> On his fair worth and single chivalry.   (IV. iv. 148–150)

The next scene (IV. v) opens with the Greeks addressing
to the same occasion. Up until now the Greeks have been a
quarrelsome lot, but as IV. v opens, Agamemnon's and
Ajax's speeches are set in an heroic, full-flowing mode,
almost out of keeping with their characters as so far presented. Indeed, the first eleven lines reflect a mood that has
appeared only once before: when Aeneas initially delivered
the challenge. This is the mood befitting Robin Hood, Little
John, and the knights and ladies of merry old England. But
the mood is broken by the entrance of Cressida, who is
certainly not the Maid Marian of romance. She is received,
and the combat gets under way. But hardly begun, it is
halted. Although Ajax wishes to continue, Hector refuses
on the ground that,

> The obligation of our blood forbids
> A gory emulation 'twixt us twain.   (IV. v. 122–123)

He goes on to say that if he could separate his cousin Ajax's
Grecian blood from his Trojan he would destroy what was
Greek,

> but the just gods gainsay
> That any drop thou borrow'dst from thy mother,
> My sacred aunt, should by my mortal sword
> Be drained! Let me embrace thee, Ajax.   (IV. v. 132–135)

Ajax's answer seems humble and human:

> I thank thee, Hector.
> Thou art too gentle and too free a man.
> I came to kill thee, cousin, and bear hence
> A great addition earned in thy death.   (IV. v 138–141)

Either Ajax has been cured of his foolish pride and the point
not emphasized, or Shakespeare has allowed his earlier characterization of Ajax to slip away unnoticed. In this new,
gracious tone he asks Hector to visit the Greek camp, and

Hector accepts, for he is anxious to see the principal warriors. Thus, the apparent climax of the plot comes to nought.

When Hector meets Achilles in the Greek camp the plot
undertakes what seems to be a new and more fitting climax:
Achilles suddenly promises to seek out Hector the next day
in battle. But Shakespeare immediately removed this prom-
ise of true climax when he opened the very next scene (V. i)
with Achilles being reminded in a letter from Hecuba of
his pledge to remain out of combat because of his love for
Polyxena, and we still remain uncertain as to where the plot
will go. The middle action then closes with the masterfully
managed scene in which the audience watches Thersites
watching Ulysses and Troilus watching Diomedes seduce
Cressida (V. ii). Because all the characters speak, little emotion is generated; on the other hand, the intellectual stimuli
of the scene, because of its depth and variety, are powerful
indeed.

Although the central action concerns the seduction, the
audience does not observe that action from a single point of
view because Ulysses, Troilus, and Thersites — who suggested to Harold S. Wilson "the degrees of reason, will, and
debased appetite in man" [7] — are on stage also observing the
action and acting as a kind of chorus. The stage is quickly
set. Diomedes enters and calls Cressida out from her father's
tent. Ulysses and Troilus then enter and stand aside, slightly
separated from each other. And finally Thersites enters and
also stands aside, but completely separated from Ulysses
and Troilus. While Troilus observes Cressida and Diomedes,
Ulysses observes all three, and Thersites observes all four. A
sample of the dialogue can best illustrate the scheme and its
effect.[8] Throughout Cressida tries to play the coquette, but
Diomedes has taken her measure and wants but one thing,
and that without persiflage. When she tries to dally, he starts
to go:

Cressida. Guardian! Why, Greek!

Diomedes. Foh, foh! adieu. You palter.

Cressida. In faith, I do not. Come hither once again.

Ulysses. You shake, my lord, at something. Will you go?
   You will break out.

Troilus.   She strokes his cheek!

Ulysses.   Come, come.

Troilus. Nay, stay. By Jove, I will not speak a word.
   There is between my will and all offences
   A guard of patience. Stay a little while.

Thersites. How the devil luxury, with his fat rump and
potato finger, tickles these together. Fry, lechery, fry!

                                        (V. ii. 47–57)

As the pattern is repeated Cressida slowly gives in, Troilus'
agony increases, Ulysses' amazement grows, and Thersites'
amusement bursts all bounds. When she finally capitulates,
Troilus cannot comprehend at first what has taken place:

                   there is a credence in my heart,
   An esperance so obstinately strong,
   That doth invert th' attest of eyes and ears,
   As if those organs had deceptious functions
   Created only to calumniate.
   Was Cressid here?   (V. ii. 120–125)

The hard, latinate diction shows his will to disbelieve, but
Ulysses' reply cuts through all delusion: "I cannot conjure,
Troyan."

Finally, Aeneas enters and separates the lovers for the
second time, now taking Troilus from Cressida after this
scene which has inverted the situation of the same morning.
That scene had ended with a reference to Hector, so also
here Aeneas says that "Hector by this is arming him in
Troy"; however this time he is not going to meet Ajax but,
as he thinks, Achilles. A deflated, distracted, and embittered
Troilus bids Ulysses adieu and the middle action of the play

closes with Thersites' scathing commentary on what has just taken place: "Lechery, lechery! still wars and lechery! Nothing else holds fashion. A burning devil take them!" (V. ii. 195–197).

THE FINAL ACTION AND THE PROBLEM OF STRUCTURE

The final action begins with the last scene at Ilium (V. iii), in which Hector cannot be dissuaded from arming by his wife, father, and sister, nor can Troilus be dissuaded from arming by his brother. Ordinarily a scene of familial debate and of heroic preparation for battle should afford the means of building toward a natural, noble climax; however, here, as so often in the play, potential structural effectiveness has been dissipated because Shakespeare has previously shown that Achilles has changed his mind about meeting Hector. Thus the audience views still another scene more with ironic detachment than with emotional engagement. This ironic sense is further reinforced by our previously having seen Troilus and Paris and Achilles each withdrawn from the battlefield because of love for his particular lady.

When Hector finally breaks away, and Troilus starts to follow, shouting defiance against Diomedes, Pandarus enters and stops him with a letter from Cressida. While Troilus reads, Pandarus fills the time with an aimless prattle concerning his failing health, then asks, "What says she there?" Troilus answers in disgust and despair:

> Words, words, mere words, no matter from the heart;
> Th' effect doth operate another way.   (V. iii. 107–108)

The Quarto scene ends here, but the Folio continues:

> *Pand.* Why, but heare you.
> *Troy.* Hence brother lackie; Ignomie and shame
>   Pursue thy life, and liue aye with thy name.   (sig. ¶¶₆)

The words are appropriate; structurally the love plot is over and the rest of the action will be concentrated in the field. As for character, Troilus' disillusionment has been complete and after his present outburst this dismissal of the go-between follows naturally. And as for the thought of the play, when Cressida proved untrue, Pandarus was to assume his new title of pander. Although the words, of course, appear again in a slightly different form at the end of the play in both the Quarto and the Folio when Pandarus appears inexplicably in the middle of the battlefield to speak his epilogue, the prose which we find there fits here, for the lines are a continuation of his present talk about his failing health and show his lack of any real feeling for either Troilus or Cressida. Still the actual epilogue of couplets could only be said at the end of the play.

The resolution of the play on the battlefield is so disparate and disjointed that editors have snipped the scene into seven small ones (and some have then turned around to say that Shakespeare never wrote such short, inconclusive snippets!). But it is a single scene, chaotic to be sure, yet moving steadily to a determined end, the death of Hector which will lead to the fall of Troy and the end of this war of "honor." [9] Because the scene in general does move in fits and starts, the death is naturally anticlimactic, but two specific elements especially mute the effectiveness of the conclusion. First, after the death of Patroclus, Achilles and Hector meet in what could have been the climax of the play, but Hector lets Achilles depart in peace because he is easily winded, being out of condition. This "fair play" by Hector is the kind that ended the trial with Ajax, is what Troilus has called "fool's play," and prepares us for the irony of Hector's actual death. The nature of this death and its aftermath are the second reason for the dramatic discomfort afforded by the conclusion: it is the result of a planned gang-murder and has none of the dignity which even Suffolk in 2 *Henry VI* and Macbeth are allowed. When Achilles enters with his Myrmidons to find Hector at rest, examining his newly won armor, his words have an ominous tone, but as he continues, ignoring Hector's simple plea of "I am unarm'd; forgo this vantage, Greek," his words become raucous, angry, and dishonest:

> Strike, fellows, strike! This is the man I seek.
> So, Ilion, fall thou next! Now, Troy, sink down!
> Here lies thy heart, thy sinews, and thy bone.
> On, Myrmidons, and cry you all amain,
> "Achilles hath the mighty Hector slain." (V. viii. 10–14)

As both armies sound retreats for the night this "great and complete man" exits with lines better fitting a Dracula than a Homeric warrior:

> The dragon wing of night o'erspreads the earth,
> And, stickler-like, the armies separates.
> My half-supp'd sword, that frankly would have fed,
> Pleas'd with this dainty bait, thus goes to bed.
> Come, tie his body to my horse's tail;
> Along the field I will the Troyan trail. (V. viii. 17–22)

When Agamemnon and the rest enter in processional (V. ix), they hear the rumor of Hector's death at Achilles' hand, and Ajax, the new man, gives a fitting epitaph:

> If it be so, yet bragless let it be.
> Great Hector was as good a man as he. (V. ix. 5–6)

To the audience, which has just seen what has taken place, this is packed with irony. Agamemnon then adds the coda to the Greek story:

> March patiently along. Let one be sent
> To pray Achilles see us at our tent.
> If in his [Hector's] death the gods have us befriended
> Great Troy is ours, and our sharp wars are ended.
> (V. ix. 7–10)

At the beginning of the story in the Greek camp, Ulysses asked a rhetorical question which indicated the main source of the Greek troubles:

> When that the general is not like the hive,
> To whom the foragers shall all repair,
> What honey is expected?   (I. iii. 81–83)

Agamemnon still hesitates to exercise the "specialty of rule," and it is not clear that the resultant "envious fever" which Ulysses described has been driven from the Greek camp. Troy will fall, but of her own weakness not because of Greek strength.[10]

The Greeks' processional is replaced (V. x) by the Trojans', Aeneas shouting aloud,

> Stand, ho! yet are we masters of the field.
> Never go home; here starve we out the night.   (V. x. 1–2)

The audience knows that this encouragement is given in vain. The Trojans know it when Troilus enters and announces starkly, "Hector is slain." Although Troy is doomed, he preaches defiance to the last. He then formally brings the Ilium story to a close:

> Hector is gone.
> Who shall tell Priam so? or Hecuba?
> Let him that will a screech owl aye be call'd
> Go in to Troy, and say there "Hector's dead":
> There is a word will Priam turn to stone;
> Make wells and Niobes of the maids and wives,
> Cold statues of the youth, and in a word
> Scare Troy out of itself. But march away.
> Hector is dead; there is no more to say.   (V. x. 14–22)

His public utterance made, Troilus makes his private one before the army departs. Had Shakespeare ended the love story in the same manner in which he introduced it, this

speech would have been about Troilus' faithfulness in the
face of Cressida's falsity. Such a speech, however, would have
completely drained Troilus of all nobility; instead, Shakespeare showed that the fire of revenge has burned out the
fire of love. Troilus seeks only Achilles:

> thou great-siz'd coward,
> No space of earth shall sunder our two hates;
> I'll haunt thee like a wicked conscience still,
> That mouldeth goblins swift as frenzy's thoughts.
> Strike a free march to Troy! With comfort go.
> Hope of revenge shall hide our inward woe.   (V. x. 26–31)

Organically, the play should end here, and textual evidence
implies that in the first version it did. But even in that version Troilus' speech would not give the play a resolute
ending: Troilus speaks with a bitterness that is brittle rather
than resonant. And *Troilus and Cressida* in its two extant
forms is still more unsatisfying in its final effect because
they each show Pandarus suddenly and inexplicably appearing on the battlefield at nightfall:

> *Pandarus.* But hear you! hear you!
> *Troilus.* Hence, broker, lackey! Ignomy and shame
>   Pursue thy life and live aye with thy name!   (V. x. 32–34)

Pandarus is labeled for all a pander and the love plot is
completed.

Pandarus stays on stage and tries to blunt the sharpness
of his dismissal. First he mumbles about his aged, aching
bones, then tries to generalize his situation, and finally turns
fully to the audience to deliver the epilogue, which by its
nature adds a final note of unrest and incompleteness to the
play, the cumulative experience of which does not provide
the usual Shakespearean repose, whether of comedy, of
tragedy, or of history. Alfred Harbage is correct in observing

that "here, and here only, in Shakespearean drama are the false and the treacherous riding high on Fortune's wheel at the end, while the honorable and true are at its base," but it is not merely the story which creates a condition of unrest.[11]

Although the plot brings its three lines to a unified conclusion, Shakespeare, as W. W. Lawrence pointed out, "never quite seems to let himself go, to allow the action to sweep him on to an inevitable climax." [12] What forces the false starts and quick stops in the story is a plot designed to display numerous moods and a variety of rhetoric rather than to build to a natural climax and a clear resolution. The love plot ends bitterly in a strange fashion of forsaking, the theme of honor is shown to be as empty as the armor taken by Hector, the Greeks never solve the problem of internal disorder, and all of these aspects of the play which tend to create the flattening uncomfortable final effect are helped along by the voices of Thersites throughout and Pandarus at the end. The rather negative action and ambivalent characterization of *Troilus and Cressida* force us to interpret the motifs of love and lust, war and honor, and order and disorder in a pessimistic manner. Even the two general themes which embrace the themes of each plot-line have a rather resigned wistfulness to them: there can be no true moral worth without ethical endorsement, and man's fallen nature is subject to the ravages of Time. These are, respectively, the general concerns of comedy and tragedy; however, this play is neither. When Thersites says that "war and lechery confound all," he suggests compactly the three dominant themes and plot-lines. War confounds the honor of Troy, lust confounds Troilus, and the Greek forces are disordered by the ravages of both. War and lechery generally confound all, but this over-all theme has no general or universal ring as developed in the play. To evoke general affirmation in response to such a theme, a play as a comedy may show people confused by war and lust working their way through to rest, harmony, and balance; or else a play as a tragedy may show people in harmony and balance, disturbed by the evils of war and lechery, and restored to harmony and balance only after war and lechery have been purged by violence and death. Neither happens in *Troilus and Cressida*; it opens in confusion and merely moves through more confusion to less confusion. If it is, as W. W. Lawrence believed, "an experiment in the middle ground between comedy and tragedy in which experience often places us," [13] it is not entirely successful because the flux of life as mirrored in the play is not sufficiently ordered or differentiated.

On the other hand, there is clear indication that the play was carefully wrought even if not well-wrought; in spite of the series of anticlimaxes, the actual ending is foreshadowed in the very beginning. The play opens at Pandarus' house and introduces in consecutive scenes the story of Troilus and Cressida, but the opening words spoken by Troilus show the audience that the love affair takes place within a context of war:

Call here my varlet; I'll unarm again.
Why should I war without the walls of Troy
That find such cruel battle here within? (I. i. 1–3)

The question points inward and Troilus' character is indeed the subject of the scene, but Aeneas at the end of the scene brings news from "the field" which recalls Troilus from reverie to matters at hand, and at one point within the scene, at the sound of an alarum, Troilus is able to react to public concerns:

Fools on both sides, Helen must needs be fair
When with your blood you daily paint her thus!
(I. i. 93–94)

Just as the first scene gives glimpses beyond its own setting, so also does the second, which continues the love plot now by introducing Cressida in colloquy with Pandarus. But her preliminary conversation with her page Alexander includes references to the occupants of Ilium, to the battlefield, and to "the Greeks"; and when Alexander says that Ajax has angered Hector, the fact points to the middle action, but the speech ominously foretells the final action:

> He chid Andromache and struck his armourer;
> And, like as there were husbandry in war,
> Before the sun rose he was harness'd light,
> And to the field goes he, where every flower
> Did as a prophet weep what it foresaw
> In Hector's wrath.   (I. ii. 6–11)

Thus, the problem of structure may be succinctly stated: why would Shakespeare consciously create an inconclusive plot?

THE SHAKESPEAREAN PRECEDENT

If Meres believed that ability to dramatize a complex story was the necessary prerequisite for a good plot, when we recall the *Robert, Earl of Huntington* plays we can understand why he praised Anthony Munday for his plotting. If this inference is correct, then at least in Meres's eyes, the *Henry VI* plays, *Titus Andronicus*, and the earliest comedies are well plotted. The action in each, regardless of its complexity, moves in a single direction toward a given end, but, as his talent in comedy increased, Shakespeare allowed underplots to move in contrasting directions to the main plot. Moreover, first in *A Midsummer Night's Dream* and then more expertly in *Twelfth Night*, he wove three plots together.[14]

On the other hand, depth was achieved with increasing

effectiveness in *Romeo and Juliet, Julius Caesar*, and *Hamlet*
— along with *Titus Andronicus*, the only tragedies written
before *Troilus* — not so much by intricate plotting as by
giving the action an informing, philosophical frame of reference. One may or may not agree that the philosophy presented through the Chorus and Friar Laurence is too removed from the personalities of Romeo and Juliet and is too
deeply involved in the character of Hamlet for either of
their plays to achieve the full psychological impact of
tragedy; however, the case of *Julius Caesar* is less debatable.
Clearly the public fall of the proud titular hero was intended
mainly to provide occasion for Brutus' private tragedy. The
informing philosophy of the play is introduced early, and
introduced through the main figures. The play builds masterfully through Brutus' temptation, the death of Caesar,
and Mark Antony's handling of the crowd. However, as
anarchy sets in, the structure of the action mirrors the theme
of disorder all too well. As a result the last part of the play
tends to run downhill inconclusively, obscuring the moral
predicament of Brutus. Academically it is easy to point out
where Brutus fell into a logical fallacy and what the significance is of Caesar's ghost, but it is hard to feel anything other
than that time ran out on a very fine person. Thus, if *Troilus*
moves in the direction of tragedy but does not produce a
tragic effect, that Shakespeare had not settled on a tragic
mode by 1601 is an important historical fact to help us judge
the conclusion of *Troilus* more sympathetically.

Shakespeare's Lancastrian cycle is of especial interest because of the structural variations which can be observed in it.
The bucket metaphor coined by Richard to depict his fall
and Bolingbroke's rise in *Richard II* surely reflects Shakespeare's conscious creation of a plot appropriate to the story,
characters, and themes of the play. Although the structure
is simple, it is sound and effective. More complicated, but

still effective is the plotting of *1 Henry IV* which is like that of *Troilus and Cressida*: three separate plot-lines move steadily toward each other, finally joining in a battle scene. Here, the plot is well handled, for each part has the final battle clearly in view from the middle of the play on, and the battle successfully resolves all parts of the story.[15] Indeed, the tavern scenes are so attractive that we tend to wish that this plot-line did not have to take Falstaff out of his element in order to reveal his cowardice on the battlefield.

Furthermore, *1 Henry IV* is a history play; it is about real events and real people. Hence, it carries with it a gratuitous atmosphere of activity off-stage. In contemporary life, when one is told "Time Marches On" or "You Are There" the barest amount of activity can stand for the most complex events because memory is called upon to support and supplement imagination. While Hal is in the tavern we "know" that the king is in council and we can "feel" Percy stirring in the North. This overarching sense of things happening simultaneously is one of the significant marks that distinguish the history play from comedy and tragedy.

2 Henry IV diverges from the genre of the history play both in its searching thoughtfulness concerning the King's destiny and Hal's duty, and in its comic underplot of Falstaff and his fellows. Henry's important scene ("Uneasy lies the head," III. i), Henry's and Hal's together ("Why doth the crown lie there upon his pillow?" IV. iv), and Hal's alone ("This new and gorgeous garment, majesty," V, ii) all have the psychological and philosophical seriousness of stately tragedy. At the same time, the comedy of low-life moves on its own plane. After Hal moves entirely out of the Falstaff plot and into the serious one, which occurs early in the play, the two lines tend to move away from each other. The Lord Chief Justice is a device to pull the two together; nevertheless, by the end of the action, there is a structural separation which may support the motif of "I know thee not old man," but which weakens the over-all effect of the play.

Henry V is the most chronicle-like of the history plays after *1 Henry VI*. Both move pageant-like through episode after episode of English history, ending with a rousing chorus of "God Save the King." Yet *Henry V*, paradoxically, is the most self-consciously produced of all Shakespeare's plays. The Chorus over and over again apologizes for the inherent limitations of the theater when one tries to represent real people and real events. He asks the audience to recall "true things by what their mockeries be" (IV. Prol). The physical reality of the stage is a support to comedy and an anchor to tragedy, but Shakespeare almost seems to realize that the stage is merely a neutral medium for realism. Although the stage is no hindrance to any kind of drama, it is important to note that Shakespeare, except for his part in *Henry VIII*, never again used recent British history as the material for a play. About this same time, as C. L. Barber has argued in *Shakespeare's Festive Comedy*, Shakespeare had developed his early art of comedy to its highest point, and was ready to explore new veins. Thus the testimony of the canon would indicate that by 1600 Shakespeare was consciously experimenting with structure, looking for a mode of focusing more directly on the involved question of character, moral choice, and ethical reverberation.

THE THEATRICAL SETTING

Shakespeare was not alone in his experimentation with plot. Indeed a clear feature of many plays from 1598 through 1603 is a lack of attention to structure, and, as M. C. Bradbrook reminds us, Ben Jonson "in his three Comical Satires [*Every Man out of his Humour, Cynthia's Revels,* and *Poetaster*] . . . almost dispensed with the intrigue; like the modern discussion play, they relied upon character and rhetoric alone." [16] In fact Jonson was so proud of his innovation of what John J. Enck has called the principle of "discontinuity" that he used it as the basis for ridiculing Anthony Munday, the popular playwright.[17] In a piece added in 1601 as an Induction to *The Case is Alterd* for performance at Blackfriars, Jonson has Munday brag:

> Why looke you sir, I write so plaine, and keepe that old *Decorum*, that you must of necessitie like it; mary you shall haue some now (as for example, in plaies) that will haue euery day new trickes, and write you nothing but humours: indeed this pleases the Gentlemen: but the common sort they care not for't, they know not what to make on't, they looke for good matter, they, and are not edified with such toyes . . . I care not for the Gentlemen I, let me haue good ground, no matter for the pen, the plot shall carry it.

It would be wrong to assume from Jonson's attack that sound plotting was entirely neglected, as *Antonios Reuenge* and *The Two Angry Women of Abingdon*, two diverse witnesses, certainly prove. However, *Histrio-mastix*, *Jacke Drums Entertainment*, *The Wisdome of Doctor Dodypoll*, and *Sir Giles Goosecap* are all patchwork. The plots of *What You Will*, the *Maydes Metamorphosis*, and *The Family of Love* are simple and quite obvious. Yet these are some of the plays which carried the private theaters to initial success from 1598 to 1603. Furthermore, the one play most obviously connected with the *Poetomachia*, *Satiromastix*, which played both publicly and privately, contains a jumble of plot-lines: the satiric Horace plot filled with *ad hominem* invective, the comic wooing of Widdow Mineuer, and the tragicomedy of the Terill family. If people came to see the attack on Jonson, did they pay attention to the rest? A safe conjecture is that they did, for unless Dekker knew his audience could and would maintain simultaneous interest in several plots, he would not have wasted time and effort trying to tie in the Horace plot. A timely rebuttal to *Poetaster* was needed and could have been offered separately in lieu of a jig had the audience not been willing to accept a play of mixed plot elements. A safe conclusion, then, is that sound plotting was not necessary for success in this particular period of transition and flux in London's theatrical world; novelty was sufficient to draw an audience.

CONCLUSION

John J. Enck has demonstrated that "about 1600 Shakespeare and Jonson took a wary professional notice of each other," and has suggested that the structure of *Troilus and Cressida* is one which follows Jonson's experimental principle of discontinuity.[18] Certainly no play in the canon before *Troilus* ends in defeat of all normal expectations, in spite of Shakespeare's use of various kinds of structure and various ways of bringing thematic concerns to bear on plot. We could say that because the sources of the stories of Troy and Troilus go on beyond the play, no particular ending is structurally suitable to a play which treats only part of a whole legend. We could argue further that the stories of the siege and the lovers were so well known that Shakespeare did not have to show the beggary of Cressida, the deaths of Troilus and Achilles, and the fall of Troy. But the fact remains that there is no handling of the Troy legend before Shakespeare's which does not try to point the story with some kind of moral or ethical observation. The sources may be responsible for the facts that make up the ending of *Troilus*, but the same sources emphasize that Shakespeare made no attempt to shape his material so that it would carry thematic reverberations outside of the play.

In both the *Iliad* and the medieval legend, Hector and

Ajax had fought in single combat; however, that Aeneas should visit the Greek camp with a challenge from Hector, that the challenge should be presented in a chivalric manner, and that Ulysses should arrange for Ajax to be selected to answer the challenge are all new in Shakespeare. Shakespeare, then, consciously or unconsciously is responsible for the feeling of frustration that is created when the trial by arms comes to naught. Furthermore, only Shakespeare shows that Andromache and Priam are unable to dissuade Hector from fighting, and his depiction of Hector's death is a unique combination of details from Homer, Lydgate, and Caxton. If the plot has no central momentum, it must have been on purpose. Even though the history of Troy goes on beyond the limits of the play, Shakespeare did not have to close inconclusively with Pandarus; he could have given Hector a noble death at the hands of Achilles and allowed a sad, but wiser Troilus to close the play in a dignified manner. Furthermore, in *1 Henry IV* Shakespeare successfully handled three plot-lines that were so resolved in a final battle scene that the play can stand alone, even though Shakespeare may have had a sequel in mind while he was writing it. The inference is inescapable that Shakespeare deliberately weakened the structural effectiveness of *Troilus and Cressida*. The answer to the problem of the plot-without-plot of *Troilus and Cressida* is that the structure of the play is both personally experimental and consciously designed to please the gentlemen. But the question remains whether or not Shakespeare provided sufficient "good matter" to please the "common sort."

CHAPTER V · THE CONCERNS
OF LOVE AND LUST

*B*Y THE END OF *Troilus and Cressida* there is no
doubt what Pandarus is: he is neither ambiguous nor
complex. But Troilus is the one and Cressida is the
other, and by the end Troilus' question asked in the first
scene may not have been fully answered:

> Tell me, Apollo, for thy Daphne's love,
> What Cressid is, what Pandar, and what we.
> Her bed is India; there she lies, a pearl;
> Between our Ilium and where she resides,
> Let it be call'd the wild and wand'ring flood,
> Ourself the merchant, and this sailing Pandar
> Our doubtful hope, our convoy, and our bark.
>
> (I. i. 101–107)

Here we can see Shakespeare preparing the foundation for
his characterization of the three main figures in the love
story, for he recognized instinctively that each had an established existence within rhetoric — Pandarus as a noun and
verb, Troilus and Cressida as the bases of automatic similes,
"as true as . . ." and "as false as . . ." — indeed, we have
already noted how the assignation scene ends with an emblematic presentation of the rhetorical roles of each. Their
plot could be called the amplifying of three tropes. But the
full traditional conception of each character could not be
presented until the end, and Shakespeare had to give them
lives of their own within the play. And because he was
Shakespeare, not all have agreed just what the lives of
Troilus and Cressida were like. Careful attention to the way
in which he drew their characters from the beginning should
dispel confusion. Then, an examination of Shakespeare's

previous handling of lovers and the concerns of love and lust ought to point up the facts that Cressida is a unique addition to the canon, that Troilus is ambiguous, and that the thematic resolution of the love plot is indefinite. But an examination of lovers and the love themes in competing plays ought to bring an answer to the problem of the love plot.

THE PROBLEM OF THE LOVE PLOT

At the outset a casual question from Pandarus sets off a speech which begins the establishment of Troilus' character:

> The Greeks are strong, and skillful to their strength,
> Fierce to their skill, and to their fierceness valiant;
> But I am weaker than a woman's tear,
> Tamer than sleep, fonder than ignorance,
> Less valiant than the virgin in the night,
> And skilless as unpractis'd infancy.   (I. i. 7–12)

The initial two lines of well turned *gradatio* show that Troilus knows his *oratio*, and the sequent hyperbolic periphrasis, the elements of which are neatly balanced with their antecedents, confirm the suggestion of a love of rhetoric for its own sake. Then follows the dialogue of *doubles-entendres* on "grinding" and "bolting," which serves mainly to suggest the character of Pandarus: a Polonius under the hot Aegean sun.

The self-conscious hyperbole of youth and aphoristic tediousness of age can produce dialogue, but not conversation. Hence the speeches that follow are spoken by Troilus and Pandarus almost back to back, the natural differences between the speakers being emphasized by the two media in which they speak.[1] Each goes on in his own manner until Troilus interrupts and finally shouts the old man down, "O Pandarus! I tell thee Pandarus —" and in his hyperbole complains at length about the aggravated "gash that love has given" him. Pandarus, unable to compete in debate, plays the hurt confidant, sulks, pouts, and seeks to withdraw, refusing to be reconciled. Alone Troilus waxes at length on his love for Cressida, but finally is interrupted in his reverie by Aeneas, "that," as W. M. T. Nowottny observes, "(like the interruptions of Pandarus) being the only way, it would seem, of checking the inexhaustible fecundity of Troilus's poetic invention." [2]

If Troilus is in love with his own words, Cressida is in love with her own wit. Even the dialogue with her page Alexander at the opening of the next scene (I. ii) reveals her character. When Alexander begins his long, comic description of Ajax with the assertion that Ajax is "a very man per se/ And stands alone," Cressida answers wittily, "So do all men, unless they are drunk." Had she stopped there, she would have displayed the quick wit of a Beatrice, but Cressida adds after drunk, "sick, or have no legs." The enumeration presses the humor out of the retort, and a smirk seems to replace a smile on the speaker's face.

But as Pandarus enters, a small touch gives dimension to Shakespeare's portrait of Cressida. Because the rest of the scene will place her only at one remove from her uncle, mocking, teasing, and delighting in light irony, Shakespeare had her take notice of Pandarus' entrance by saying aloud to Alexander "Hector's a gallant man": she knows that her uncle comes only to praise Troilus. Finally a retreat is sounded, and the action of the scene becomes the parade of the Trojan soldiers "as they pass toward Ilium." The action, of course, serves to introduce the main Trojans and to sound out Cressida's true emotions concerning Troilus; but the situation is as humorous as any in the play. If Pandarus proved sufficiently prominent to warrant a place on the second title page of the Quarto, it was not so much because of his short epilogue as a scene like this in which his garbled, excited remarks about each of the warriors keeps the attention on the speaker, rather than drawing it to the Trojans. Still — in spite of his humor — we are not allowed to forget that Pandarus is merely a fashionable courtier, never in itself a recommendation in Shakespeare, and an old, foolish one to boot. As to the courtier who accosts Hotspur, to Pandarus common soldiers are but "Asses, fools, dolts! chaff and bran, chaff and bran!" Hence, when he describes Troilus using terms which define the basic qualities of traditional, optimistic humanism,[3] he does so casually, without recognition of the values implied. The nature of Cressida's retorts continues the revelation of her kind of wit:

> *Pandarus.* . . . Is not birth, beauty, good shape, discourse, manhood, learning, gentleness, virtue, youth, liberality, and suchlike, the spice and salt that season a man?
> *Cressida.* Ay, a minc'd man! and then to be bak'd with no date in the pie, for then the man's date is out.
> *Pandarus.* You are such another woman! A man knows not at what ward you lie.
> *Cressida.* Upon my back, to defend my belly . . . If I cannot ward what I would not have hit, I can watch you for telling how I took the blow, unless it swell past hiding, and then it's past watching.   (I. ii. 275–295)

Cressida is not a widow as in Chaucer; were she, she would have Shakespeare's usual justified privilege for such remarks.[4]

Although Cressida has been full of mockery and teasing, Pandarus has understood her true desire; their parting exchange is direct and devastatingly clear:

> *Pandarus.* I'll be with you, niece, by-and-by.
> *Cressida.* To bring, uncle?
> *Pandarus.* Ay, a token from Troilus.
> *Cressida.* By the same token, you are a bawd.   (I. ii. 304–307)

After his exit, Cressida speaks indirectly to the audience through a series of weakly aphoristic couplets.[5] Sounding like a Restoration coquette, she confesses her love for Troilus, but says in part:

> That she belov'd knows naught that knows not this:
> Men prize the thing ungain'd more than it is.
>
> . . . .
>
> Then, though my heart's content firm love doth bear,
> Nothing of that shall from mine eyes appear.
>
> (I. ii. 314–321)

These two, Troilus and Cressida, could hardly be worse matched. He is all words and passion; she, all irony and calculation.

Before the lovers are brought together Troilus' passionate nature is further revealed in the council scene at Ilium. But the concerns of war and honor seem to bring out a different side of Troilus' nature — or perhaps we are more used to his special kind of bluster in response to public questions. Certainly it is this aspect of Troilus which Ulysses describes in IV. v. Because Ulysses speaks more wisely and accurately than any other character in the play, and we must believe that Ulysses speaks what he honestly believes, many critics typified by L. L. Schücking feel that we should take Ulysses' sketch of Troilus as authoritative and reliable. Such a response is further encouraged by the fact that only thirty lines intervene between Ulysses' description of Cressida, which coincides with the impression that she has created, and his sketch of Troilus. Although this coincidence seems like natural pairing, what has not been realized is the great difference between the two sketches. When Ulysses describes Cressida she has just skippingly kissed the Greek host, and what Ulysses describes is what we have just seen — it is almost a stage direction to one playing Cressida's role because of its emphasis on appearance, on externals:

There's language in her eye, her cheek, her lip;
Nay, her foot speaks. Her wanton spirits look out
At every joint and motive of her body.
O, these encounterers so glib of tongue,
That give accosting welcome ere it comes
And wide unclasp the tables of their thoughts
To every ticklish reader — set them down
For sluttish spoils of opportunity
And daughters of the game!   (IV. v. 55–63)

In contrast, what Ulysses says of Troilus is merely a repetition of what Aeneas had told him seven years before, and much of what he says simply does not coincide with what we have seen of Troilus in love and Troilus in council. When Agamemnon asks "What Troyan is that same that looks so heavy?" Ulysses replies:

The youngest son of Priam, a true knight;
Not yet mature, yet matchless; firm of word;
Speaking in deeds and deedless in his tongue;
Not soon provok'd, nor being provok'd soon calm'd;
His heart and hand both open and both free,
For what he has he gives, what thinks he shows,
Yet gives he not till judgment guide his bounty,
Nor dignifies an impair thought with breath;
Manly as Hector, but more dangerous;
For Hector in his blaze of wrath subscribes
To tender objects, but he in heat of action
Is more vindicative than jealous love.
They call him Troilus, and on him erect
A second hope as fairly built as Hector.
Thus says Aeneas, one that knows the youth
Even to his inches, and with private soul
Did in great Ilion thus translate him to me.
                                              (IV. v. 96–112)

The one speech is eyewitness; this is hearsay. Furthermore,

two dramatic factors weaken its reliability: the speech is a filler during a spate of action before the trial by arms, and Shakespeare's making clear to us what Ulysses thinks at this point in the play about both Cressida and Troilus sets up and heightens the effect of the scene which follows outside Calchas' tent. Still the speech cannot be ignored. On the other hand, because it does contain contradictory elements, debate over Troilus' character cannot center on it but must consider the evidence found in the entire play.

Certainly his soliloquy which opens the assignation scene (III. ii) would seem to give the lie to the claim that Troilus never "dignifies an impair thought with breath"; in fact, Alfred Harbage has said that this much interpreted speech contains "the most sensual lines" in Shakespeare: [6]

> I am giddy; expectation whirls me round.
> Th' imaginary relish is so sweet
> That it enchants my sense. What will it be
> When that the wat'ry palates taste indeed
> Love's thrice-repured nectar? Death, I fear me;
> Sounding destruction; or some joy too fine,
> Too subtile-potent, tun'd too sharp in sweetness
> For the capacity of my ruder powers.
> I fear it much; and I do fear besides
> That I shall lose distinction in my joys,
> As doth a battle when they charge on heaps
> The enemy flying.   (III. ii. 19–30)

This is not, as O. J. Campbell believes, the speech of a practiced sensualist, nor does it recapture, as E. M. W. Tillyard believes, the aura of Romeo's innocent, young romanticism.[7] There is more sensuality here than is usual in virginal expectation, especially since chastity is more a state of mind than a physical condition; yet there is an admission of physical innocence which it would be folly to deny.[8] What should be recognized is that Troilus combines abstract relish and real anticipation in such a way that the speech is both speculative and sexual.[9]

The way that the scene develops, the speculative dominates even though at first it would seem to be the sexual: after much leering, hand-rubbing excitement, Pandarus finally leads in Cressida, and the lovers fall into a long embracing kiss, the only one in Shakespeare. All his other stage kisses are the shortest sort, if only because of the all-male casts, and usually emotion is expressed verbally by his lovers. But here they are silent while Pandarus describes their kiss in what might be called a stage-direction that takes at least thirty seconds to speak. Thus when the kiss is over and Troilus the orator says, "You have bereft me of all words, lady," it would be hard if not impossible to speak the line without evoking laughter. Pandarus immediately starts to talk again in his excited, suggestive manner, while they start to kiss again.

After Pandarus' exit to prepare for their retirement, Cressida speaks her first words, "Will you walk in, my lord?" It would seem that the lady wished to get to the business at hand, but Troilus cannot miss the chance for rhetorical effusion: "O Cressid, how often have I wish'd me thus!" Cressida, after two long embraces, is confused; she starts to say that the opportunity is here for real indulgence, but she breaks off: "Wish'd, my lord? The gods grant — O my lord!" There follows then a kind of circular, lovers' stichomythia in prose; his conversation is all on the abstract plane, hers on the concrete. He postulates that in love "the desire is boundless and the act a slave to limit"; she replies that all lovers merely "have the voice of lions and the act of hares." Troilus retorts in prose of the highest style: latinate, royal, aphoristic, rhythmic, balanced. Yet after this outburst Cressida simply asks, "Will you walk in, my lord?"

Before Troilus can begin another speech Pandarus enters,

asking with the audience, "Have you not done talking yet?" Troilus reaffirms his steadfastness and Pandarus speaks for Cressida: "Our kindred, though they be long ere they be wooed, they are constant being won. They are burrs, I can tell you; they'll stick where they are thrown" (III. ii. 117–120). His last statement will certainly prove true, and lest we believe his first, Shakespeare had Cressida confess that,

> Prince Troilus, I have lov'd you night and day
> For many weary months.
> *Troilus.* Why was my Cressid then so hard to win?
> *Cressida.* Hard to seem won; but I was won, my lord,
> With the first glance that ever — pardon me!
>   (III. ii. 122–126)

To have gone on to a full and open confession would have been in the manner of Julia, Juliet, and Rosalind. But Cressida is not frank and innocent. She breaks off, and the masterful speech which follows reveals the complicated nature of this Shakespearean heroine who, because she is both an honest woman and dishonest lady, has caused so much trouble for critics.[10] She tries to leave, petulantly excusing herself in Donne-like terms which are similar to those that Troilus employs at the end of the love affair:

> I have a kind of self resides with you;
> But an unkind self, that itself will leave
> To be another's fool. I would be gone.
> Where is my wit? I know not what I speak.
>   (III. ii. 155–158)

When Troilus taunts her with, "Well know they what they speak that speak so wisely," we are reminded of his interest in rhetoric; as a result, when the high-termed exchange that follows concludes with Troilus' saying,

I am true as truth's simplicity
And simpler than the infancy of truth,   (III. ii. 176–177)

it is difficult to feel any depth of sincerity, for we know, as
we know when we listen to Marlowe's Leander present
himself to Hero in a similar manner (l. 208), that we are in
the presence of a self-conscious orator.

In the parting scene of the next day (IV. ii) Troilus' lack
of wit and abundance of fancy as well as Cressida's opposite
characteristics are further shown. Their dialogue alternates
between the casually mundane and the almost lyrical: [11]

> *Troilus.*   Sleep kill those pretty eyes,
>   And give as soft attachment to thy senses
>   As infants empty of all thought!
> *Cressida.*   Good morrow then.
> *Troilus.* I prithee now, to bed.
> *Cressida.*   Are you aweary of me?   (IV. ii. 4–9)

Troilus quiets her with a comment on the shortness of the
night, and she agrees that it "hath been too brief," which
gives him a chance for further lyrical display:

> Beshrew the witch! with venomous wights she stays
> As tediously as hell, but flies the grasps of love
> With wings more momentary-swift than thought.
> You will catch cold, and curse me.   (IV. ii. 12–15)

This last line is not so humorous as it is deadening and tends
to destroy the potential emotion in the lovers' parting. Cressida's discordant, pettish complaints add to the flattening
effect: "Prithee tarry. /You men will never tarry." After
Pandarus enters further discomfort and alienation stem from
his "naughty mocking," as Cressida calls his prurient teasing. Tempers begin to flare, Aeneas knocks on the door, and
the discord reaches its climax:

> *Cressida.* Who's that at door? Good uncle, go and see.
>   My lord, come you again into my chamber.

> You smile and mock me, as if I meant naughtily.
> *Troilus.* Ha, ha!   (IV. ii. 36–39)

Pandarus tries to put Aeneas off, but Troilus returns to see what is the matter. When told, he does not display the fire which might have been expected (and which Dryden had to invent for this turning point in the love plot):

> *Troilus.* Is it so concluded?
> *Aeneas.* By Priam and the general state of Troy.
>   They are at hand and ready to effect it.
> *Troilus.* How my achievements mock me!
>   I will go meet them; and, my Lord Aeneas,
>   We met by chance; you did not find me here.
>   (IV. ii. 68–73)

"O gods, how you do plague me!"; "expectation whirls me round"; "How my achievements mock me!" — psychologists must have some term for this habit of evasion and shifting of responsibility.[12]

Because Troilus lacks wit or depth, the audience is able to judge him directly; because Cressida is complex, Shakespeare had to exploit her lack of imagination to develop through irony the grounds for evaluating her. When she finds that she must go to the Greeks, her response would be touching — were it not for the fact that she is not legally married:

> I will not, uncle. I have forgot my father;
> I know no touch of consanguinity,
> No kin, no love, no blood, no soul so near me
> As the sweet Troilus.

And Shakespeare further controlled the audience's response as Cressida continues,

>   O you gods divine,
> Make Cressid's name the very crown of falsehood
> If ever she leave Troilus!

Whatever emotion her words may have worked is purpose-
fully dissipated by this undramatic use of dramatic irony;
the rest of her speech, however, is masterfully ambivalent:

> Time, force, and death,
> Do to this body what extremes you can,
> But the strong base and building of my love
> Is as the very centre of the earth,
> Drawing all things to it.   (IV. ii. 102–111)

Cressida obviously means her soul, and because of our orien-
tation within the laws of Newtonian gravity, we may forget
that for Elizabethans the center of the earth was the dregs
and waste material of creation — that area most separate
from God, worth less than even the smallest stone on earth.

Even if this point is too subtle, by the end of the scene
outside Calchas' tent there should be no doubt in Troilus'
mind concerning "What Cressid is," but the question he
asked Apollo at the beginning of the play about himself is
not so easily resolved. After Cressida chooses to submit to
Diomedes because, in Ulysses' earlier words to Achilles, the
"present eye praises the present object," Troilus will not
have it so:

> Let it not be believ'd for womanhood!
> Think we had mothers. Do not give advantage
> To stubborn critics, apt, without a theme
> For depravation, to square the general sex
> By Cressid's rule. Rather think this not Cressid.
>   (V. ii. 129–133)

Even though he is beginning to understand Cressida, Troilus separates himself from the cynical cavilers like Thersites
who call all wives and mothers whores as he slowly moves
from disbelief, through recognition of fact, to rejection of
Cressida and hate for Diomedes. The transitions take place
slowly, but in emotionally packed verse which does not so

much show reasoning as it does the elusive motion of the
mind as it comes to grips with a problem, agonizingly
grapples, and finally triumphs. His speeches paraphrase
easily, but lose in summary the pressure of felt experience.
He first posits that Cressida is goodness, with all its neo-
Platonic implications. Yet, he recognizes the truth of what
he has seen; therefore, there is no other conclusion but that
she is not goodness. His retreat from a kind of pathetic, sub-
jective idealism is graphically summed up:[13]

> Instance, O instance! strong as Pluto's gates:
> Cressid is mine, tied with the bonds of heaven.
> Instance, O instance! strong as heaven itself:
> The bonds of heaven are slipp'd, dissolv'd, and loos'd;
> And with another knot, five-finger-tied,
> The fractions of her faith, orts of her love,
> The fragments, scraps, the bits, and greasy relics
> Of her o'ereaten faith, are given to Diomed.
>
> (V. ii. 153–160)

Because Ulysses has been told that Troilus is "Not soon provoked" and that he lets "judgment guide," he cannot understand either Troilus' present rage or how "sluttish" Cressida
could be the cause; his concern also might be heightened by
the fact that he has heard that Troilus "being provoked [is
not] soon calmed" and that "he in heat of action / Is more
vindicative than jealous love." The audience has reason to
believe that Troilus is *easily* provoked and *not* guided by
reason; yet his next speech illustrates that Aeneas has properly evaluated Troilus in anger. He pledges his hate in
vengeance upon Diomedes and concludes with one last outburst:

> O Cressid! O false Cressid! false, false, false!
> Let all untruths stand by thy stained name,
> And they'll seem glorious.   (V. ii. 178–180)

At last he knows "What Cressid is." To what degree he knows himself is unclear; he is certainly sad, but he is not much wiser.[14]

The best commentary on the nature of the love story and Troilus' final mood can be taken from an exchange between Ulysses and Troilus after Hector and the Trojans have been welcomed into the Greek camp. Troilus has asked where Calchas lives and if Ulysses will conduct him there after Agamemnon's feast. Ulysses has agreed, but further asks,

> of what honour was
> This Cressida in Troy? Had she no lover there
> That wails her absence?   (IV. v. 287–289)

We know what Ulysses thinks of Cressida and of Troilus; hence, this question falls naturally from his lips. Troilus' answer is revealing:

> O, sir, to such as boasting show their scars
> A mock is due. Will you walk on, my lord?
> She was belov'd, she lov'd; she is, and doth;
> But still sweet love is food for fortune's tooth.
>
> (IV. v. 290–293)

When Romeo says, "He jests at scars that never felt a wound," the metaphorical expression for the effect of love is couched in a sentence that implies ridicule of the lover by someone inexperienced in love. Here we have the same metaphor describing the effect of love, but this time we are forced to view the lover from a position of cynical experience, "A mock is due."

The problem of the love plot is, then, why did Shakespeare create such mismatched lovers, and seem to make such a depressing comment on love?

THE SHAKESPEAREAN PRECEDENT

The love story of Proteus and Julia in *The Two Gentlemen of Verona*, even to the exchange of love tokens, is the story of Troilus and Cressida in reverse. These lovers, however, are younger. Julia may call her nurse Lucetta "a goodly broker" when she delivers Proteus' letter and she may even seem to agree with Cressida that

> maids, in modesty, say "no" to that
> Which they would have the profferer construe "ay"!
>
> (I. ii. 55–56)

But she is an innocent, modest maiden, who realizes that chastising her nurse is "churlish," and that Cressida's coquettish philosophy is "wayward." In self-criticism she concludes:

> My penance is, to call Lucetta back
> And ask remission for my folly past.   (I. ii. 64–65)

If we smile at Julia's youthful seriousness it is with approbation.

Proteus, true to his name in word and deed, is not so engaging. One scene in particular should be noticed. After Proteus has seen Silvia, he rationalizes his predicament in a way that reveals a self-aware amusement which is similar to Cressida's detachment; his speech affords a sharp contrast to Troilus' passionate logic-chopping in the council scene and semiconscious awareness of logic after observing Cressida's faithlessness:

> Unheedful vows may heedfully be broken,
> And he wants wit that wants resolved will
> To learn his wit t'exchange the bad for better.
> . . . .
> I to myself am dearer than a friend,
> For love is still most precious in itself;
> . . . .
> I cannot now prove constant to myself
> Without some treachery us'd to Valentine.   (II. vi. 11–32)

The syllogism is perfect, but not valid. Yet youth is resilient and all the lovers rebound into the proper arms.

Lysander in *A Midsummer Night's Dream* also affords a contrast to Troilus. Upon awakening to see Helena after Puck has rubbed his eyes with the magic potion, he courts her in a coldly intellectual manner:

> The will of man is by his reason sway'd
> And reason says you are the worthier maid.
> Things growing are not ripe until their season;
> So I, being young, till now ripe not to reason;
> And touching now the point of human skill,
> Reason becomes the marshal to my will
> And leads me to your eyes; where I o'erlook
> Love's stories, written in Love's richest book.
>
> (II. ii. 115–122)

Had Troilus spoken this way he would not have become involved with Cressida — for more reasons than one!

One of "Love's" stories was her encounter with Adonis, and in Shakespeare's telling of the myth Adonis has the youthful intellectualism of Proteus and Lysander; but Venus is reduced to a pun: "She's Love, she loves, and yet she is not lov'd" (l. 610). It is this light vein that makes Shakespeare's satire on lust not only delightful but effective. From the beginning Venus is ridiculous in her Amazonian overtures:

> Here come and sit, where never serpent hisses,
> And being set, I'll smother thee with kisses.   (ll. 17–18)

Such insipience points up the barrenness of her desire, and her way of speaking is not unlike Cressida's grand manner.

Sexual desire, certainly, forms part of Romeo and Juliet's love; however, Shakespeare departed from his sources in reducing their ages, so that the young lovers could be shown in innocence.[15] Although their love is natural and sincere,

the way in which it began is ominous. The Chorus before
Act II speaks in a detached manner as he mocks Romeo's
sudden change of heart:

> Now old desire doth in his deathbed lie,
> And young affection gapes to be his heir;
> That fair for which love groan'd for and would die,
> With tender Juliet match'd, is now not fair.
> Now Romeo is belov'd, and loves again,
> Alike bewitched by the charm of looks;
> But to his foe suppos'd he must complain,
> And she steal love's sweet bait from fearful hooks.

This suggests more than love at first sight; it implies an
evaluation of such love. Gaping young affection, bewitching
looks, and love stolen from hooks do not bode well.

Romeo is too young to know what conscience is, but Friar
Laurence supplies the wisdom concerning "grace and rude
will" which Romeo lacks and without which he cannot hold
self-debate. For example, Friar Laurence is quick to moral-
ize on Romeo's change:

> So soon foresaken? Young men's love then lies
> Not truly in their hearts, but in their eyes.
> Jesu Maria! What a deal of brine
> Hath wash'd thy sallow cheeks for Rosaline!
>   .   .   .   .
> *Romeo.* Thou chid'st me oft for loving Rosaline.
> *Friar.* For doting, not for loving, pupil mine.   (II. iii. 67–82)

Impetuous though they are, Romeo and Juliet insist on marriage before they consummate their love; nevertheless, the
irrational basis of that love is never completely compensated.
Juliet does not realize the inherent danger in calling Romeo
"the god of my idolatry."

The love affairs in *Love's Labour's Lost* bear little analogy
to the loves of either Troilus and Cressida or Romeo and

Juliet because the play deals comically with older lovers who know just what they are going about. Thus, the comic detachment necessary to distinguish between illusion and reality is established within the play so that it is both amusing and true when the love-struck Berowne says,

> This is the liver vein, which makes flesh a deity,
> A green goose a goddess — pure, pure idolatry.
> God amend us, God amend! we are much out o' th' way.
>
> (IV. iii. 74–76)

In the light of this kind of evidence, it is clear that Shakespeare would have Hector's and Ulysses' words on true worth applied to Troilus in love.

A middle ground of love between the extremes of Romeo's youthful passion and Berowne's mature playfulness is found in *The Merchant of Venice*, where the loves of Lorenzo and Jessica, Bassanio and Portia yield further positive evidence of how Shakespeare would have the audience judge the love of Troilus for Cressida. Because Lorenzo falls in love with a Jewess, Shakespeare was especially careful to show that the love is no mere whim. Hence Lorenzo's words to the plain-speaking Gratiano give a sound definition of what may be considered as worthy love:

> Beshrow me but I love her heartily;
> For she is wise, if I can judge of her;
> And fair she is, if that mine eyes be true;
> And true she is, as she hath prov'd herself;
> And therefore, like herself, wise, fair, and true,
> Shall she be placed in my constant soul.   (II. vi. 52–57)

The basis of Hector's challenge was that Andromache was "wiser, fairer, truer" than any Grecian lady. These are, indeed, the attributes that constitute Shakespeare's ideal for woman.[16]

Needing to show that Portia measures up to this ideal,

Shakespeare would have impugned her virtue had he not handled the casket scene deftly. He had only this one, short scene in which to develop her love for Bassanio as sound and true. Because of the expectation and delight shown by the two lovers, this scene has been cited by T. W. Baldwin, in the *Variorum*, as a parallel to the assignation in *Troilus and Cressida*. But what is so striking here is that bewitching gazes and imaginary relish are tempered and muted. Charged diction was needed in order to show that Portia wants this wooer to win her as well as to keep the casket selection suspenseful; yet Shakespeare met this necessity without detriment to Portia's character:

> O love, be moderate; allay thy ecstasy;
> In measure rain thy joy; scant this excess!
> I feel too much thy blessing. Make it less
> For fear I surfeit! (III. ii. 111–114)

About the only similarity between Troilus and Bassanio is that they use the same adjective, "giddy"; how Bassanio uses the word points up the difference between them. After choosing the proper casket, he says that he stands,

> Giddy in spirit, still gazing in a doubt
>
> . . . .
>
> whether what I see be true,
> Until confirm'd, sign'd, ratified by you. (III. ii. 144–148)

Troilus is too absorbed in abstract thought to be thus controlled by reality. Like Romeo, he has a touch of the poet, but Troilus' vein is questioning and theorizing, while Romeo's is accepting and generalizing. Troilus' use of rhetoric is more nearly akin to that of the self-conscious Richard II.

Even though Troilus' predicament at the end of the play is similar to Claudio's in *Much Ado*, Troilus does not reach the same depths of passionate anguish and disillusion.

Claudio denounces Hero's seeming dishonesty not briefly and bluntly but in rich and sensuous terms:

> you are more intemperate in your blood
> Than Venus, or those pamp'red animals,
> That rage in savage sensuality.   (IV. i. 60–62)

He is so disillusioned that he, like Troilus' "stubborn critics," begins to doubt the divinity of beauty and the chastity of women:

> Thou pure impiety and impious purity!
> For thee I'll lock up all the gates of love,
> And on my eyelids shall conjecture hang,
> To turn all beauty into thoughts of harm,
> And never shall it more be gracious.   (IV. i. 105–109)

Claudio, in fact, is as voluble, if not as copious, as Hamlet in crying out on lust.

One strange aspect of *Troilus and Cressida* is that lust seemingly goes undamned as well as unpunished. The rest of the canon is not so indefinite. Suffolk's adulterous lust for Margaret is punished in *2 Henry VI* and is framed in an interesting metaphor. As he departs for France to escort Margaret to England, Suffolk closes *1 Henry VI* by saying that he goes

> As did the youthful Paris once to Greece,
> With hope to find the like event in love
> But prosper better than the Troyan did.
> Margaret shall now be Queen, and rule the King;
> But I will rule both her, the King, and realm.
>
>   (V. v. 104–108)

And the metaphorical picture is completed by Edward in *3 Henry VI* when he curses Margaret by saying that

> A wisp of straw were worth a thousand crowns,
> To make this shameless callet know herself.

Helen of Greece was fairer far than thou,
Although thy husband may be Menelaus;
And ne'er was Agamemnon's brother wrong'd
By that false woman as this king by thee.   (II. ii. 144–149)

Edward is in no position to cast moral aspersions; when he
woos Lady Grey he is blunt, lewd, and even brags about his
having fathered many bastards (III. ii). Richard chastises
his brother for his uncontrolled bestial appetite, but one of
the master strokes that make this "foul lump of deformity"
come alive in *Richard III* is the lascivious smile and crude
sexuality that pervade his manner when he talks of love. Of
all the crimes, moral and ethical, that Tamora is guilty of in
Titus Andronicus it is her beast-like lust that is presented as
the justification for her death.

I have picked these examples of display and condemnation
of lust from the very early plays, for Theodore Spencer suggested in *Shakespeare and the Nature of Man* that Shakespeare only shows a concern for lechery with *Hamlet* and
after. On the contrary, he dramatized from the beginning
the moral problem of lust; however, he was never personally
didactic on the subject, but treated the matter in keeping
with the various decorums of the various plays. If we should
need to reconfirm our trust in Shakespeare's morality after
reading *Troilus and Cressida*, perhaps it would be more
profitable to look in his nondramatic productions for indica-
tions of his felt beliefs. Even here we do not meet the poet
face to face, but at least we do not have first to account for
the various decorums involved in creating drama.

When Shakespeare treated Venus lightly in *Venus and
Adonis*, he answered one of the demands of the fashionable,
Ovidian genre in which the poem was written. On the other
hand, if Adonis appears ridiculous it is a weakness in artistic
execution, for, in spite of the genre, it is clear that Shakespeare wished to portray in Adonis a serious young man, of

whom it truly could be said "To grow into himself was his desire" (l. 1180). He asks Venus to

> Measure my strangeness with my unripe years.
> Before I know myself, seek not to know me.   (ll. 524–525)

The pun may create an awkward ambivalence, but the primary thought is serious and sincere. In fact, even when Shakespeare used exaggerated diction in order to satirize Venus, the seriousness usually reserved for Adonis sometimes crept in:

> And having felt the sweetness of the spoil,
> With blindfold fury she begins to forage.
> Her face doth reek and smoke, her blood doth boil,
> And careless lust stirs up a desperate courage,
>   Planting oblivion, beating reason back,
>   Forgetting shame's pure blush and honour's wrack.
> (ll. 553–558)

In spite of the serious turn at the end of this stanza, *Venus and Adonis* is mostly a source of delight, not instruction; but *Lucrece* because of its intensely serious didacticism is diametrically opposed. The high seriousness of both the council scenes in *Troilus* is achieved by Shakespeare's use of basic philosophical concepts to wrestle with public problems; here the seriousness is intensified by the application of those basic concepts to personal problems. "Doting Tarquin," like Troilus, is one of those who

> all for want of wit,
> Make something nothing by augmenting it.   (ll. 153–154)

Because Tarquin is more intelligent than either Troilus or, so far as we know him, Achilles, he is able to supply both sides that are necessary for an internal debate, whereas it takes a Hector and a Ulysses to complement publicly the ideas of Troilus and Achilles. Tarquin knows that he

Is madly toss'd between desire and dread:
Th' one sweetly flatters, th' other feareth harm;
But honest fear, bewitch'd with lust's foul charm,
   Doth too too oft betake him to retire,
   Beaten away by brainsick rude desire.　　(ll. 171–175)

The debate goes on concerning the two kinds of fear and the traditional demands and functions of appetite, will, and reason. He concludes that

My will is strong, past reason's weak removing.

.　　.　　.　　.　　.　　.　　.　　.　　.　　.

Affection is my captain, and he leadeth.

.　　.　　.　　.　　.　　.　　.　　.　　.　　.

Then childish fear avaunt! debating die!
Respect and reason wait on wrinkled age!　(ll. 243, 271–275)

He wavers in his resolution when he sees Lucrece's innocent beauty, yet he "dotes on what he looks, 'gainst law or duty" (l. 497). Her pleas avail not and lust surfeits itself. Afterward, Tarquin's attitude in self-recrimination is like that in many of Shakespeare's sonnets.

Although we do not know when they were written or in what order, Meres's mention of the sonnets in 1598 and their general pertinence offer sufficient historical and critical justification for bringing them into this review of the canon leading up to *Troilus.* Any of the sonnets which deals with the conflicting demands of reason and will in love sheds helpful light on the play, but two in particular treat themes which are raised by the love plot. Because Sonnet 129, "Th' expense of spirit," contains a stronger statement than the play ever makes on the ravages wrought by "lust in action," and Sonnet 147, "My love is as a fever," embraces the corrective self-knowledge that mere "desire is death" which Troilus does not attain, they provide useful Shakespearean gauges by which the conduct of the lovers and the character of Troilus may be measured.

Diana wooed by Bertram in *All's Well* affords a final interesting comparison to the love affair of Troilus and Cressida. Here we also have a march of soldiers, but while it passes, Diana and her friends assert themselves clearly on the side of honesty against the "engines of lust" (III. v. 21). In the actual wooing scene her forthright nature stands in direct contrast to Bertram's (and Cressida's as well):

> 'Tis not the many oaths that makes the truth,
> But the plain single vow that is vow'd true.   (IV. ii. 21–22)

In this scene, honor receives a double definition. Bertram believes that honor is an inherited attribute, in this case symbolized by his family's ring which has been "bequeathed down from many ancestors" (43). Diana's retort defines that honor which is woman's defense against lust:

> Mine honour's such a ring;
> My chastity's the jewel of our house,
> Bequeathed down from many ancestors,
> Which were the greatest obloquy i' th' world
> In me to lose. Thus your own proper wisdom
> Brings in the champion Honour on my part
> Against your vain assault.   (IV. ii. 45–51)

No such concept of honor appears in *Troilus* simply because Helen and Cressida are not chaste.

THE THEATRICAL SETTING

Although Marston's interlude of "Troilus and Cressida" in *Histrio-mastix* is the only direct handling of the story extant from the immediate period of Shakespeare's play, Mall Berry in Heywood's (?) *Faire Maid of the Exchange* passes from one lover to another just as does Cressida. She plights her troth to Bowdler in a mock marriage, but goes off with Barnard at the end of the play. Even though Bowdler likens his situation to that of Menelaus left by Helen and Paris, there is a great difference in that Mall not only does not sleep with Bowdler but reforms his rakish ways, as well as a small difference in that Bowdler is more like Diomedes than Troilus (pp. 71–72, 87).

At the end of Marston's *What You Will* there occurs a love encounter that is quite suggestive of Shakespeare's treatment of Troilus, Cressida, and Pandarus. Quadratus the self-confessed libertine has miraculously seduced Lampatho from the melancholy scholarly life and introduced him to the gay Meletza. After a long, witty speech, Lampatho is obliquely warned by the courtly lady that "slow speech, swift love doth often shrowd." Like Cressida she knows what she wants, but Lampatho continues in a rhetorical vein and the three voices sound familiar:

> *Lampatho.* My soul's intranc'd your favor doth transport
>   My scence past scence, by your adored graces,
>   I doat, am rapt.
> *Meletza.* Nay, if you fall to passion and past scence,
>   My breasts no harbor for your love, go packe, hence.
> *Quadratus.* Uds fut thou gull, . . .
>   My soul's intraunc'd, fut couldst not clip and kisse?
>
>   (pp. 280–281)

Shakespeare's lovers, in contrast, are not held in ridicule, if only because Chaucer's serious story holds a control over the tone of Shakespeare's play. An even clearer use of Chaucer's story than Shakespeare's is, as T. M. Parrott has shown, in George Chapman's *Sir Giles Goosecap*.[17] Chapman presents the first meeting of the lovers, "Troilus'" confession of his infatuation, and the exchange of letters; he even follows Chaucer in the setting for the first assignation. However,

Chapman's characterizations and his unromantic but "happy" ending are quite different from Chaucer's. Parrott felt that Clarence is "a scholarly prig" in his cold calculation of love as a needed safety valve for the pressures of analytic thought, and that Eugenia is "an Elizabethan *grande dame*," a young widow with intellectual pretensions. It might be said that Shakespeare's independent use of Chaucer begins where Chapman's leaves off, the overlap occurring in the heroes' speeches of expectation. Both use abstract, latinate diction and talk about their love in a philosophical mode, but Troilus speculates about the physical aspects of love and Clarence about the mental:

> My lord, I feel a treble happiness
> Mix in one soul, which proves how eminent
> Things endless are above things temporal
> That are in bodies needfully confin'd:
> I cannot suffer their dimensions pierc'd,
> Where my immortal part admits expansure,
> Even to the comprehension of two more
> Commix'd substantially with her mere self.   (IV. iii. 5–12)

Romeo and Juliet seems to have had great influence on love scenes at the turn of the century. It is certainly apparent that Marston conceived his Katherine and Pasquil in *Jacke Drums Entertainment* to be similarly innocent lovers. But the intended atmosphere of innocence is weakened when Katherine says that she comes to Pasquil "As the fierce Fawcon stoupes to rysing fowle." She is more like Cressida when she all but invites Pasquil to bed without waiting for marriage; however, Pasquil hopes that she may find "Peace to thy passions." The similarity to Shakespeare's love plot in *Troilus* continues inasmuch as Pasquil is typified "as bare as naked Truthe" and their love is pledged in a sweeping manner:

Katherine. When I turne fickle, vertue shall be vice.
Pasquil. When I prove false, Hell shall be Paradice.
(pp. 198–200)

In a way he does prove false because he runs away when her face is disfigured by "doting" Mamon. In the *Tryall of Chevalry,* Prince Philip displays the opposite attitude when he pledges to marry Bellamira even though Rodoricke has destroyed her beauty. It is interesting to note that in expectation of seeing her he, like Troilus, experiences "a kind of killing extasie," but he is able to control himself until the end of the play, at which time their marriage helps to restore peace between France and Navarre (pp. 299, 355).

Jonson's Ovid and Julia share a love which, O. J. Campbell states, is "frankly wanton in tone," a tone which "permeates every portion" of *Poetaster*;[18] nevertheless, Horace says that the banquet which celebrates their love is "innocent mirth, / And harmlesse pleasures, bred, of noble wit" (IV. vii. 41–42). When Ovid must part from the imprisoned Julia, his "noble wit" is employed in trying to convince her not to commit suicide, for without her body he cannot love her. He freely confesses that he dotes on the follies of the flesh:

I am mad with loue.
There is no spirit, vnder heauen, that workes
With such illusion: yet such witchcraft kill mee,
Ere a sound mind, without it, saue my life.   (IV. ix. 99–102)

Although Campbell has called Ovid "almost pathetic" in this scene of parting,[19] when Deliro shows his doting humor in *Every Man out of his Humour,* it is clear that Jonson wished him to be ridiculous. In either case, the language of dotage is the same:

O, MACILENTE, I haue such a wife!
So passing faire, so passing farre vnkind,

But of such worth, and right to be vnkind,
(Since no man can be worthy of her kindness.)

(II. iv. 28–31)

Albius, the citizen husband in *Poetaster*, receives even stronger ridicule for loving his wife so much that he is blind to her courtly pretensions. In contrast, in Dekker's *Old Fortunatus*, the Prince of Cyprus realizes that Princess Agripyne is a coquette and he is sorry that he dotes on her (III. ii. 195); Shakespeare's Troilus is not so clear-sighted.

Nor is he as calculating as Gerardine in Middleton's *The Family of Love*, although both lovers have similarly abstracting minds:

This is the chamber which confines my love,
This is the abstract of the spacious world:
Within it holds a gem so rich, so rare,
That art or nature never yet could set
A valued price to her unvalued worth.   (I. ii. 54–58)

Although in their trysts, pledges, and partings Gerardine and Maria are patterned, as W. J. Olive has demonstrated, after Romeo and Juliet, the attitude toward love which they reveal is quite different.[20] Maria consents to fornication with the rapidity of Cressida, and even though she becomes pregnant there is but one oblique reference to marriage in the play. As Glister unwittingly prepares to conduct Gerardine, who is hidden in a trunk, to his niece, his ironic words reveal the light attitude which Middleton held with regard to the conduct of this love affair: "By this time my humorous lover is at Gravesend; and I go with more joy to fetch his trunk than ever the valliant Trojans did to draw in the Grecian jade: his goods shall into the walls of my Troy, and be offered to a face more lovely than ever was that thrice-ravished Helen" (II. ii. 3–8).

When we remember that honest Mall Berry in *The Faire*

Maid of the Exchange also had been likened to Helen, we can see the range of attitudes expressed toward love and lust in the drama under review. Although Troilus and Ulysses comment on Cressida, Shakespeare for the most part let the audience evaluate her; it will be helpful, then, to look at some of the women in these plays in comparison and contrast to Cressida in order to see what attitudes toward love and lust they assume.

Directly opposite to Cressida in attitude and station is Jane in Dekker's *The Shoemakers Holiday*. She admits that she

> could be coy as many women be,
> Feede you with sunne-shine smiles, and wanton lookes,
> But I detest witchcraft

In her "true chaste loue" Jane would rather be Rafe's "wife, then a kings whore" (III. iv. 49–79, *passim*).

The lesson of Heywood's *1* and *2 Edward IV* would be as acceptable to Jane as it would be to Bess Momford in *The Blind Beggar of Bednal Green* by John Day; Bess also scorns "to be a Princes Concubine" (sig. G₄). Maid Marian, or Matilda, resists Prince and King John to the point of death throughout Munday's *Downfall* and *Death of Robert, Earl of Huntington*. Caelestine, Walter Terill's wife in Dekker's *Satiromastix*, is equally ready to choose death before allowing a king's lust to desecrate her love. On the other hand Marston's Rossaline, Winifred, and Meletza seem to consider marriage just another way of satisfying their lusts. When Marston has Rossaline in *Antonio and Mellida* dream out loud about a "bouncing thigh" (p. 16), he, as A. J. Axelrad observes, obviously intended Rossaline to appear ingenuous, but Axelrad points out that she "n'est pas amoureuse et paraît même avoir le coeur absolument sec." [21] Violetta in Middleton's (?) *Blurt, Master-Constable* has Fontinelle dance before her with a lady of the court so that she can watch his body in motion; her remarks are neither modest nor brief (I. i. 203ff.). After they are married and he has visited the courtesan Imperia, Violetta says that she is willing to share her husband even at the expense of her action's being called dotage (V. ii. 130).

Mall Barnes in Henry Porter's *The Two Angry Women of Abingdon* is also quite frank in her desire for a husband; she feels that going on eighteen means that she is starting to decline. Both she and her brother wonder how much longer she will be able to resist the demands of the flesh. Nevertheless, she is quite insistent that marriage and a husband are the only means of satisfaction in which she is interested (pp. 297, 328, *passim*). Princess Julia in Dekker's *Patient Grissil* is likewise quite frank; she wants neither marriage nor a husband, but she is as determined to keep her virginity as Mall is to lose hers. Still different from these two is the French lady in Heywood's *The Foure Prentises of London*, who proves that she followed Guy to the Holy Land for the sake of love, not "shameless lust," by sleeping with him for a year without revealing her sex.

Millicent Clare moves in fashionable circles in *The Merry Devil of Edmonton* (by Michael Drayton?), but upon eloping with Mouchensey she marries before the night is over. Although Lodowick in Henry Chettle's *Hoffman* is compared to "Priam's Firebrand" (l. 543) for abducting Lucibella who is called Helen, the analogy breaks down when we see them sleep chastely in each other's arms. Fredericke and Odillia elope in the anonymous *The Weakest Goeth to the Wall*, but find Sir Nicholas to marry them. He praises their avoidance of "Fornication" and "lasciuious lust," although he charmingly admits that "the flesh prickes my holy selfe now and then" (ll. 1287–1289).

On the other hand, Maria in Middleton's *The Family of*

Love seems to accept fornication as a natural extension of her love. She gives in after a token verbal hesitancy, has no regrets, and remains quite loyal to and in love with Gerardine. Their love may be immoral, but it is sincere, ending in marriage. In fact, except for common prostitutes, Cressida is the only unmarried woman in the plays of 1598 to 1603 who sleeps with two men. The closest analogies, positive and negative, are with those who are tempted to commit adultery.

Alfred Harbage has shown clearly how, from the points of view of authors and audiences, adultery was a laughing matter in the private theaters and a serious moral issue in the public ones. For example, Mrs. Brabant, Sr., cuckolds her husband in Marston's *Jacke Drums Entertainment* merely for request's sake (p. 227), whereas the refusal of Anselm's invitation under similar circumstances by Mrs. Arthur in the anonymous *How a Man May Choose a Good Wife from a Bad* is so automatic and absolute that we know without further investigation that she is the good wife (p. 75). With this distinction in mind let us glance at the thematic implications in various heroines' falls with the hope that those implications may push toward a better understanding of Cressida.

The most elevated theme is in Heywood's *A Woman Killed With Kindnesse*, where Anne's fall is not treated so much in terms of lust and love as of sin and virtue. The play reaches out ethically, so that not just the husband is affected but the whole community. A more exclusively domestic tragedy is the anonymous *A Warning for Faire Women*. Anne Saunders, like the "good wife" Mrs. Arthur, repulses Browne's first overture with great dignity, but she slowly loses all self-respect. It is even implied that before she finally repents she tries to seduce a minister. The dumb shows and "Tragedy" make it quite explicit that such is the result of chastity's being overcome by lust. Heywood's treatment of Mistress Shore in *1* and *2 Edward IV* emphasizes her desertion of her husband and her role of housewife, rather than her obvious sexual turpitude.

Henry II, in the anonymous *Look About You*, is called a "lecher" to his face because of his affair with the late Rosamond Clifford. Lady Faulconbridge tries to talk Prince Richard out of his lustful desires, Robin Hood chastises his "desire unchaste and rude," and Richard finally confesses that his lust is "respectless, reasonless" and says that he will try to reform by going to the Holy Land (pp. 414–417, 488–489). The Bastard Faulconbridge in Shakespeare's *King John* is proof of his success! But the actual sin occurs in neither play nor is it excused in either.

I have cited no thematic treatments of love and lust in plays from the private theaters simply because none is to be found, positive or negative. There is clearly a lustful note in some of the love scenes in plays written for the private theaters, but the lechery in these plays is never called anything other than simple love. In cases of adultery, if anyone is chastised it is the cuckold and not the adulterer. In fact, Jonson adds ridicule to his portrait of Fallace in *Every Man out of his Humour* by saying that she is too ugly "to be dishonest" (Preface). Only two plays from the public stages allow lust to pass by without much comment. Fuller in the anonymous *How A Man May Choose* is a former "melancholy humorist" who brags quite bluntly about a sexual conquest (pp. 17–19), and Sir John of Wrotham, "honest Jack," in Drayton's *1 Sir John Oldcastle* is allowed to wallow in "lechery" with his "lusty concubine" Doll (pp. 114, 163).

CONCLUSION

We have seen that Shakespeare always loved a lover, but displayed no simple, constantly romantic view of love before *Troilus and Cressida*. For example, there is the uncomplicated love of Julia, the full-blooded love of Juliet, the witty love of Beatrice, and the lustful love of Venus. Still, all these loves, regardless of their quality, are active; in *Troilus and Cressida* love is lethargic. The affair between Troilus and Cressida is brief, but ends in distress. Troilus from the beginning was more concerned with the idea and the formalities, Cressida with the game and the getting, than either was with the reality and the giving of love. Troilus' attitude leads inevitably to what the evolving philosophy of the canon and the specific philosophy of Hector and Ulysses call "dotage," the making of the service greater than the god. Cressida's leads to commitment to a patterned existence, to the maintenance of identity through giving in, to seeing life as a game of chess. Hence, for both the sexual act was all important, but for different reasons: for Troilus it was a new experience to be pondered philosophically; for Cressida it signified conquest, triumph. In these respects the lovers are most like those heroes and heroines in the private plays of the day who abstractly rhapsodize about love or calculatingly satisfy themselves through the act of love. And as in the love plots of Marston, Jonson, and Chapman what the world called lust is in the world of the play called love. Even though Eric Partridge finds that the play is "only slightly bawdier" than *Hamlet* and *All's Well*,[22] what distinguishes *Troilus* from its immediate neighbors in the canon and in the public theater is the lack of voices damning lust. Helen and Cressida are condemned as unworthy persons, but their mutual weakness is never called lust, except by Thersites whose indignation is anything other than righteous, and who is certainly not Shakespeare.[23]

The mere presence in the play of a Helen, a Cressida, and a Pandarus could account for this seemingly un-Shakespearean failure to chastise sin because of the emblematic quality which these figures had obtained in popular literature by

Shakespeare's day, and because Shakespeare consciously plays upon their established abstract values in order to maintain audience interest in the predetermined love plot. But working against this symbolic condemnation is the fashionable small talk which finds a kind of virtue in sexual smut and lust's debility. The bawdy of Shakespeare is usually impersonal and broadly applicable, whereas the bawdy of this play is spoken with a sense of self-conscious cleverness. It does not have that "normality and candor" which Alfred Harbage has found typical in the ribaldry in the public plays; rather it seems more in keeping with the ribaldry of the coterie plays.[24] The difference between the two kinds of bawdy can be seen by comparing the dialogue between the gentlewomen decorating the bridal hall at the opening of Dekker's *Satiromastix* with that between Rossaline and Mellida in the beginning of Marston's *Antonio and Mellida*. Such pointing is necessary, for we are dealing with comparative qualities, not measurable quantities. For example, Abbie Findlay Potts must have been led by the similarity of atmosphere in *Cynthia's Revels*, *Poetaster*, and *Troilus and Cressida* to make her study of parallel passages and verbal echoes among the three plays.[25] Her thesis that Shakespeare made a detailed use of Jonson's plays is not convincing because isolated phrases compared out of context prove little. Nevertheless, her general, unstated assumption seems quite accurate: the atmosphere of much of *Troilus* is like that of many of the private plays that we have glanced at.

The sensuous love of Ovid and Julia in Jonson's *Poetaster* finds its counterpart in the love of Troilus and Cressida, the only difference being that Troilus and Julia are interested in the theoretical side of sexual love, while Ovid and Cressida are concerned with the practical side. The licentious tone of Ovid's banquet is recreated by Helen and Paris. They, in turn, would have been amused by Hedon and Anaides in

Jonson's *Cynthia Revels* (II. ii) who rehearse *doubles-en-tendres* so that they will be acceptable to the ladies of the court who, in the opinion of O. J. Campbell, "are bound to-gether in their academy by consuming sensual curiosity."²⁶ The table talk in Chapman's *Sir Giles Goosecap* (IV. i), like the conversation between Pandarus and Cressida (I. ii), is utterly pointless. Balurdo's page in *Antonio and Mellida* (III. ii) is as clever as his master is foolish, and he uses his wit to ridicule Balurdo just as Paris' page ridicules the courtly Pandarus.

This use of a witty page by Shakespeare is strong evidence that in writing *Troilus and Cressida* he had his eye on the novel aspects of the private plays that were drawing the trade. The use of the clever servant as a means of comic in-trigue was as old as Greek comedy, and as recent as Lyly, but the chorister companies used the clever servant mainly in his other capacity as witty observer. Like a midget in a vaudeville skit, a small boy with a high voice could evoke laughter by displaying a quick wit and a sharp tongue in ridicule of his larger mates. Witty pages would do nothing to further the plot, but merely pun, jibe, and joke, all for laughter's sake. O. J. Campbell has shown that one of the features of "comicall satyre" is the giving of a character sketch by either a witty page or some other authorial spokes-man before the person described comes on stage. For ex-ample, Mercury, a page in Jonson's *Cynthia's Revels* (II. iii), so describes Crites, who is Jonson's spokesman if not the *persona* of Jonson himself, and Alexander, Cressida's witty page, describes Ajax (I. ii) in a speech which is a perfect parody of Mercury's.²⁷ If Shakespeare was imitating the theater of the coterie in *Troilus and Cressida*, it was not slavishly and blindly.

Many of the scenes in *Cynthia's Revels* are filled with what Mercury calls *"Court-decorums."* These are the word games

that are merely ways of passing the time of day when gossip
has been exhausted. Abbie Findlay Potts suggests that
Pandarus' description of Troilus' color and the allegory of
Troilus' fifty-two hairs (I. ii) may be reports of other court
games, but we can be more certain that another empty pastime is mentioned in *Troilus and Cressida*, even though we
do not see it. As Andelocia and Shadow, the younger son
and loyal servant of Dekker's *Old Fortunatus*, near the
court of England, they begin a game of "Paradoxes," which
is the building of chains of false reasoning by applying the
logical method of Ramus of puns: "A dish of Paradoxes is
a feast of straunge opinion, tis an ordinarie that our greatest
gallants haunt nowadaies, because they would be held for
Statesmen" (II. ii. 50–54). This is a favorite pastime of
Achilles and Patroclus for whom, Ulysses tells the Greek
council of war,

> All our abilities, gifts, natures, shapes,
> Severals and generals of grace exact,
> Achievements, plots, orders, preventions,
> Excitements to the field or speech for truce,
> Success or loss, what is or is not, serves
> As stuff for these two to make paradoxes.   (I. iii. 179–184)

Miss Potts suggests that when Ulysses describes Patroclus'
mocking, satiric pageants — "Which, slanderer, he imitation calls" — Shakespeare is describing Jonson's plays. The
idea is interesting, especially when it receives a kind of support that Miss Potts did not have in mind: M. C. Bradbrook
believes that Ulysses' description of these displays of "ridiculous and awkward action" (I. iii. 149) is a sound description
of the decadence of Jacobean drama with regard to the
themes and conventions of Elizabethan tragedy.[28]

Through Achilles-in-love the same atmosphere of lethargy
and amorous debility which pervades Ilium is brought into

the Greek camp. It is not so surprising, then, that within this atmosphere Thersites would accuse Achilles of homosexuality. Although we must keep in mind that it is the traditional detractor Thersites who speaks, the fact that this is the "only indubitable allusion to homosexuality in Shakespeare" in contradistinction to the many allusions in the private plays of the period is in itself another indication of Shakespeare's having been influenced by the plays on the other side of the river.[29] Still, Shakespeare's competition came from the public theaters as well, even though we have not yet found in *Troilus and Cressida* much "good matter" for the "common sort."

CHAPTER VI · THE DEMANDS OF WAR AND HONOR

*H*ECTOR NOT Achilles was to Elizabethans the true hero of the *Iliad*. He was magnanimous, wise, and manly — a true knight, one of the Nine Worthies, in spite of his being allied with a doomed people. Chivalry during the Middle Ages was a personal matter, a moral concern, and Hector's reputation could flourish in spite of Trojan folly. But to be a knight in the sixteenth century meant service to the state; in England it meant not service to a lady, but to *the* lady; and one might wonder whether or not the reputation of Hector could survive untarnished in such a context. The Hector we meet in *Troilus and Cressida* is a perfect knight, but Shakespeare did not allow him a noble, dignified death. In the light of Shakespeare's treatment even of villains, one hesitates to read criticism of Hector into the fact. But just before the actual death occur two episodes which seem by their nature to carry thematic hints with them. First Achilles and Hector meet, but Achilles is not in condition, and Hector's chivalrous nature will not let him take unfair advantage of another man, even his enemy. But these are the principles that lead to his death. Then, after Achilles exits having accepted Hector's "courtesy" with "distain," a Greek in fine armor passes across the stage, catching Hector's eye and desire. He pursues, takes the Greek, and returns to comment on what he finds:

> Most putrefied core so fair without,
> Thy goodly armour thus hath cost thy life.   (V. viii. 1–2)

Hector is no doubt a good man, but what are we to make of his way of life?

THE PROBLEM OF THE TROJAN PLOT

The Trojan plot opens with an acting out in II. ii of a grammar school debate which must have been familiar to many of Shakespeare's audience: should Helen be returned to end the war, or should she be defended out of deference to Paris' love and the Trojans' honor?[1] Priam asks Hector, the eldest son and chief warrior, for his opinion, then, except for one short speech, sits silently throughout the ensuing debate which gives shape to the thematic concern of the appropriate demands of war and honor on the state and on the individual. Yet Priam should be visualized in a central position during the scene, his head turning from one speaker to another, resembling that of a spectator at a tennis match. When the king is the observer and not the observed there arises the dangerous implication that the "specialty of rule" is being neglected within the walls of Troy just as it is in the Greek camp.

Because the debate among the sons of Priam has given rise to various critical estimates concerning Shakespeare's metaphysics, it might be well before proceeding to remind ourselves that we are dealing with a literature in which psychology is not concerned with motivation and impulse in themselves, but with the moral and ethical actions of men; hence, motivation and impulse are important only as they lead to effects outside themselves. Moral and ethical responsibility for *what* is willed is more important than *why* it is willed.

Although Hector opens with words which are to become a theme of his opposition, "Though no man lesser fears the Greeks than I," he is quick to dismiss his personal point of view in order to recall the general situation. He justifies this larger, political concern by reminding the familial council that there is a difference between ignorant, cowardly fear and knowledgeable, manly fear which is really healthy, rational respect for evaluated danger. As a result, his opinion is the blunt "Let Helen go," and his justification is that stated by Diomedes to Paris (IV. i): Helen is not worth a fraction of the lives that have been lost in her defense.

Troilus earlier seemed inclined to the same opinion, but he now interrupts Hector because to him the loss of "common" lives is nothing to "the worth and honour of a king" which he places high above "fears and reasons." Revealing his passion and love of rhetoric, Troilus goes on to play upon the lesser meanings of "fears and reasons," and powerfully concludes:

> Nay, if we talk of reason,
> Let's shut our gates and sleep. Manhood and honour
> Should have hare hearts, would they but fat their thoughts
> With this cramm'd reason. Reason and respect
> Make livers pale and lustihood deject.   (II. ii. 46–50)

Hector in disgust can only comment in the plainest manner:

> Brother, she is not worth what she doth cost
> The holding.

Undaunted, Troilus returns, "What is aught but as 'tis valu'd?" Cressida would have smiled in silent confidence, for one of her coquettish maxims is that "Men prize the thing ungain'd more than it is" (I. ii. 315). In answer to his younger brother, Hector patiently explains that

> value dwells not in particular will:
> It holds his estimate and dignity
> As well wherin 'tis precious of itself
> As in the prizer. 'Tis mad idolatry
> To make the service greater than the god;
> And the will dotes that is attributive
> To what infectiously itself affects
> Without some image of th' affected merit.   (II. ii. 53–60)

This speech of succinctly phrased commonplaces of Elizabethan thought gives the play a unifying theme, for Hector's words can be applied to each of the three plot-lines. Troilus dotes on an unworthy object, the Greek host is on the edge of chaos because will has asserted itself over reason (I. iii. 116–124), and the Trojans defend Helen who has little intrinsic worth.

Troilus tries to answer with equal calm, but his opening words are in error and take on an ironic cast: they not only are a metaphor for the Trojan situation but also are personally prophetic. As in all of the long speeches in the play, the subject is clearly stated and the conclusion indicated in the opening lines:

> I take to-day a wife, and my election
> Is led on in the conduct of my will,
> My will enkindled by mine eyes and ears,
> Two traded pilots 'twixt the dangerous shores
> Of will and judgment. How may I avoid,
> Although my will distaste what it elected,
> The wife I chose? There can be no evasion
> To blench from this and to stand firm by honour.
>
> (II. ii. 61–68)

The first four and a half lines show that Troilus even at the mature Elizabethan age of twenty-three does not know the basic assumptions of philosophy and psychology. That one's choice of an object is carried out by one's will is certainly true; the will is the executive officer. However, since even in its freedom the will should be guided by reason, the fact that the will is "enkindled by . . . eyes and ears" is no justification for action. As Hooker explained in the *Laws of Ecclesiastical Polity*, "Appetite is the Will's solicitor, and the Will is Appetite's controller; what we covet according to the one by the other we often reject; neither is any other desire termed properly Will, but that where Reason and

Understanding, or the show of Reason, prescribeth the thing desired" (I. vii. 3). Troilus has already said that he does not believe in reason; we know now that this assertion has not been mere sophistic rhetoric, for Troilus gives to will the power of choice, the traditional office of reason.

Furthermore, we have seen that when Troilus comes to "distaste" his chosen love, he does not stand firmly by her. It is easy enough to say that,

> the remainder viands
> We do not throw in unrespective sieve
> Because we now are full.   (II. ii. 70–72)

But his words return on him when his bond to Cressida is loosened and,

> The fragments, scraps, the bits, and greasy relics
> Of her o'ereaten faith, are given to Diomed.   (V. ii. 159–160)

Nevertheless, Troilus' present speech in support of his stand that the Trojans defend Helen is vividly phrased, and pushes onward with the vigor of youth. Like Cressida, Helen

> is a pearl
> Whose price hath launch'd above a thousand ships
> And turned crown'd kings to merchants.   (II. ii. 81–88)

Although he is wrong, just as Faustus was wrong, the hyperbole sounds more natural in Troilus' mouth, and in spite of error after error which can be revealed by analysis, the over-all effect of the speech is positive. Regardless of formal logic and theoretical psychology, the complex of the human heart is automatically engaged by the desire "to stand firm by honor."

Lest this voice of unreason be too persuasive, Shakespeare introduced a voice of reason in Cassandra, who is believed to be mad. The beauty of such irony is truly classical and

befitting tragedy; her words are clear and all embracing:
"Our firebrand brother Paris burns us all." Visibly moved,
as he is not when later Cassandra speaks to him, Hector asks
Troilus if Cassandra's ominous words have not worked

> Some touches of remorse? Or is your blood
> So madly hot that no discourse of reason,
> Nor fear of bad success in a bad cause,
> Can qualify the same?   (II. ii. 115–118)

Again "fears and reasons" are objectively presented. Having
no answer, Troilus can only assert that even if the outcome
of Helen's rape was bad, it still can be justified because the
honor of the Trojans makes it "gracious."

After Paris has seconded Troilus, Hector argues at some
length, in a true "discourse of reason." His speech is long
and is well known. The first eleven and a half lines quite
bluntly and correctly stamp the speeches of Paris and Troilus
as those of

> young men, whom Aristotle thought
> Unfit to hear moral philosophy.
> The reasons you allege do more conduce
> To the hot passion of distemp'red blood
> Than to make up a free determination
> 'Twixt right and wrong; for pleasure and revenge
> Have ears more deaf than adders to the voice
> Of any true decision.   (II. ii. 166–173)

Then follows the gracefully phrased, serious appeal to the
"moral laws / Of nature and of nations" (173–188) to
justify a return of Helen to her husband.[2] He points out
how the law of nature binding Helen and Menelaus has
been "corrupted through affection," and that to continue
"doing wrong extenuates not wrong." But to correct Paris
and the "great minds" that resist the law of nature and
persist in doing wrong calls for something grossly lacking

in this play: a king or "law in each well-ord'red nation" to exercise God's authority on earth. If the Elizabethan audience was sufficiently "king conscious," Priam's silence at this point could explain and justify the abrupt change of direction in Hector's speech, for he now agrees that Helen should be kept:[3]

> Hector's opinion
> Is this in way of truth. Yet ne'ertheless,
> My sprightly brethren, I propend to you
> In resolution to keep Helen still;
> For 'tis a cause that hath no mean dependence
> Upon our joint and several dignities.   (II. ii. 188–193)

Geoffrey Bush might be right when he says of Hector's switch, "Ulysses' speech is acted out; the image of order is forfeited before our eyes. It is a painful moment, when it is confessed that a mind can go one way in truth and another in resolution."[4] Or does Hector sadly shake his head knowing that in this particular incident the human spirit has acted neither wisely nor well, hoping only that this mistake will not be so serious that Troy will be prevented from profiting from its error. One thing is clear: Hector has separated the concerns of war from the concerns of honor. As a nation the Trojans are waging an evil war; as individuals they have their honor at the stake.

Troilus in glee reiterates that Helen

> is a theme of honour and renown,
> A spur to valiant and magnanimous deeds,
> Whose present courage may beat down our foes,
> And fame in time to come canonize us.   (II. ii. 199–202).

The irony here is signaled by the obvious: Troy is doomed, as the audience and Cassandra and Calchas know full well. Moreover, we have seen that an Elizabethan audience hardly

considered the Trojans as saints and that Helen was anything but a symbol of honor. Again Hector says "I am
yours," and the formal council, Hector and Helenus on
Priam's right and Paris and Troilus on his left, dissolves
into a scene of general hand shaking and back slapping. As
they exit, with no signified recognition of their father's
presence, Hector tells about his challenge sent among "The
dull and factious nobles of the Greeks." The effect of the
announcement is ambivalent: on the one hand it points forward in the plot to the middle action, but on the other it
further undercuts the elevated seriousness of the debate, a
debate which has only revealed the doubt and dedication
alike of the Trojan host on the allied subjects of war and
honor, and in the end that Hector and the Trojans have
cast their lots in favor of the pursuit of honor.

After the symbol of this pursuit and the atmosphere which
informs it are fully revealed in the next Ilium scene (III. i),
the one in Paris' apartment, the actual pursuit continues
when Hector meets Ajax in "the field" and then visits the
Greek camp (IV. v). What is noteworthy is how this scene
is not "national" or war-like, but is personal in a way that
athletic games are personal. The emphasis is not on nations
at war but individuals so that the scene comes to a natural
climax when Hector and Achilles square off and vow to
meet the next day in single combat. And fittingly the scene
closes with a call to banquet.

So far in the play Hector has been shown as a man of
public wisdom and private integrity. He is against the war,
but would not kill Ajax. In the light of these facts the last
scene in Ilium (V. iii) takes on an ironic cast, an irony
deepened by the fact that Hector thinks he is arming to
meet Achilles, who the audience knows has changed his
mind. Andromache opens by painting a Hector opposite to
the one we saw at the beginning of the play:

When was my lord so much ungently temper'd,
To stop his ears against admonishment?
Unarm, unarm, and do not fight to-day.   (V. iii. 1–3)

And Cassandra enters to help Andromache plead with Hector not to fight. When she, too, is repulsed by Hector because "The gods have heard me swear," Cassandra answers with the clarity with which she first spoke in the play. Indeed, she and Andromache make the kind of appeal that should be effective with Hector because it parallels his earlier "laws of nature and of nations" speech:

Cassandra. The gods are deaf to hot and peevish vows.
   They are polluted off'rings, more abhorr'd
   Than spotted livers in the sacrifice.
Andromache. O, be persuaded! Do not count it holy
   To hurt by being just. It is as lawful,
   For we would give much, to use violent thefts,
   And rob in the behalf of charity.
Cassandra. It is the purpose that makes strong the vow;
   But vows to every purpose must not hold.
   Unarm, sweet Hector.   (V. iii. 16–25)

Hector has had his trumpet sound already, and he tells Troilus a few lines later, "I am to-day i' th' vein of chivalry." These two instances make an interesting frame for Hector's reply to his wife and sister:

Mine honour keeps the weather of my fate.
Life every man holds dear, but the dear man
Holds honour far more precious-dear than life.
          (V. iii. 26–28)

So far the only "honor" which has been defined in the play is reputation for steel-fisted consistency in pursuing a particular course of action, regardless of its nature or probable outcome.

That this honor is a private, not a public, concept is amply shown when Troilus enters, for Hector tries to dissuade him from going to the field. Troilus ignores the plea. A man spiritually beaten and angrily defiant, he cares not what fate has in store. Hector is as set in his purpose, but his manner remains quiet. Priam enters to add his and Hecuba's warnings that "this day is ominous," and the foreboding atmosphere of sure destruction is heightened by Hector's cold and calm replies. Again, degree seems to be vizarded in Troy, for Cassandra and Andromache sense that Priam will be swayed. When they ask Hector to listen to his father, he indignantly says,

Andromache, I am offended with you.
Upon the love you bear me, get you in.   (V. iii. 77-78)

Paris, on a plea from his mistress, would refrain from battle; Hector, on a plea from his wife, will not. Such is the "love" for which Trojans exercise "honor."

The problem raised by the Trojan plot, then, can be phrased in three ways: what are the proper limits of demand placed on an individual by war and honor? Or, what are the obligations to a private oath when facing the facts of war? Or, what are we to make of Hector who can be so calm and objective with regard to the public good but so committed and egocentric with regard to his own?

THE SHAKESPEAREAN PRECEDENT

In general, as a woman's honor depends upon her maintenance of chastity, or womanhood, the Shakespearean precedent shows us that a man's honor depends on his gaining virtue, or manhood, and soldiering bravely in war is the quickest way to prove one's self. The King of France in *All's Well* points this out in praising the memory of Bertram's father, but when war is so used its ethical implications are muted:

The Florentines and Senoys are by th' ears,
Have fought with equal fortune, and continue
A braving war.   (I. ii. 1–3)

Although the king refuses to grant the official aid requested
by both parties to the war, he gives his courtiers permission
to go as individuals and fight on either side. One of his lords
is quick to praise the king's decision, because the war

> well may serve
> A nursery to our gentry, who are sick
> For breathing and exploit.   (I. ii. 15–17)

When the Duke of Florence has a brief scene in which these
basic ideas are repeated as he welcomes the French courtiers,
it is interesting to find that he has stated offstage "The
fundamental reasons of this war" (III. i. 2). We are forced
to take it on faith that "Holy seems the quarrel" (4). In
this way war per se is kept in the background, just as it is
when the honors gained by Benedick are discussed in *Much
Ado*.

On the other hand, the *Henry VI* plays bring the ugly
facts of war out into the open. There is nothing romantic
about Joan of Arc's army, Jack Cade's mob, or the father
in *3 Henry VI* who, having killed his own son, swears that
he is as full of sorrow,

> Even for the loss of thee, having no more,
> As Priam was for all his valiant sons.   (II. v. 119–120)

Talbot in *1 Henry VI* may challenge the French to fight like
gentlemen (III. ii. 70) and he may gain much honor in
France because his victories are achieved in support of the
English cause, yet even his attitude toward war is not entirely appealing:

> Pucelle or Pussel, Dolphin or Dogfish,

Your hearts I'll stamp out with my horse's heels
And make a quagmire of your mingled brains.

(I. iv. 107–109)

The chivalrous approach to personal honor which necessarily puts the ethical concerns of war and policy in the
background and the realistic approach to war which makes
honor a secondary, derivative concern both appear in *Richard II*. Shakespeare so exploited these contrasting attitudes
in designing his plot, characterizations, and themes that the
ways of chivalry are measured against the ways of policy.
But just as neither Richard nor Bolingbroke is drawn simply
in blacks and whites, so also the contrasting philosophies are
depicted without a final relative evaluation.

The demands of private honor and public policy in the
conduct of war are also interestingly brought together in
2 Henry IV. When the forces of Prince John are outnum-
bered, he agrees to talk to the chief rebels, and he swears
"by the honour of my blood" to redress the grievances which
the Archbishop of York has presented. When John suddenly has the rebel leaders arrested after their forces have
been dismissed, Mowbray asks, "Is this proceeding just and
honourable?" and the Archbishop asks, "Will you thus break
your faith?" They seem rightly to be shocked by a breach
of truce under the rules of war. But Prince John does not
suddenly change his mind; he has been conducting a carefully planned stratagem:

I promis'd you redress of these same grievances
Whereof you did complain; which, by mine honour,
I will perform with a most Christian care.
But for you rebels — look to taste the due
Meet for rebellion and such acts as yours.   (IV. ii. 113–117)

Prince John does not break the chivalrous rules of war; he
ignores them. By working on other grounds he maintains

personal honour and yet ends a bad war in the most expeditious manner. There is no satire on chivalry here; rather Shakespeare seems to take it for granted, as in all of his history plays, that the rules of chivalry simply are inadequate, hence inapplicable, to the conduct of general warfare.[5]

In *Henry V*, an assumption that chivalry has its limitations underlies the king's gentle baiting of Captain Fluellen. But the captain is not a ridiculous figure; he is merely old-fashioned. To him, "It is the greatest admiration in the universal world, when the true and aunchient prerogatifes and laws of the wars is not kept," for he lives by "the ceremonies of the wars, and cares of it, and the forms of it, and the sobriety of it, and the modesty of it" (IV. i. 66–75). With his love of order and his chivalry, Fluellen is a comic combination of Ulysses and Hector, and there is a touch of regret in the king's voice as he praises the captain:

> Though it appear a little out of fashion,
> There is much care and valour in this Welshman.
>
>   (IV. i. 85–86)

The king knows that abstract rules cannot blunt the sharp realities and pressing demands of war. It is certainly out of practical necessity and not as the scourge of God that the king has the French prisoners killed. We should not feel that this is dishonorable; no practical means of ending warfare as expeditiously as possible are ever criticized in Shakespeare. This is not to say that Shakespearean precedent would seem to justify the way in which Achilles has Hector slaughtered because Hector's death is a means of ending the Trojan war. On the contrary, regardless of the size and validity of the war, individual integrity must be maintained in man-to-man combat.

The line of distinction between the permissible demands

of war and honor is illustrated well in *1 Henry IV*. When Vernon counsels Hotspur not to become engaged with the king's forces until the rebels can be at full strength the next day, the Douglas accuses him of cowardice. Vernon replies in a manner similar to Hector in council that

> If well-respected honour bid me on,
> I hold as little counsel with weak fear
> As you, my lord, or any Scot that this day lives.
>
> (IV. iii. 10–13)

The demands of honor, nevertheless, do not override the demands of sound policy. When the Douglas still insists that battle be waged that night, Vernon answers,

> Come, come, it may not be. I wonder much,
> Being men of such great leading as you are,
> That you foresee not what impediments
> Drag back our expedition.   (IV. iii. 16–19)

Hotspur, of course, is so strongly influenced by a desire "To pluck bright honour from the pale-fac'd moon," that he holds policy in contempt, calling it "base and rotten." But Prince Hal's thoughts before the final battle illustrate how honor and policy may be exercised in a complementary manner. He tells Worcester realistically,

> In both our armies there is many a soul
> Shall pay full dearly for this encounter,
> If once they join in trial.   (V. i. 83–85)

Then he seems to turn romantic as he goes on to praise Hotspur's "noble deeds," while confessing that he himself has "a truant been to chivalry." But his final statement logically resolves the two attitudes:

> And [I] will, to save the blood on either side,
> Try fortune with him in a single fight.   (V. i. 99–100)

This challenge is followed by Falstaff's famous "catechism" on honor, which reinforces the Shakespearean differentiation between war and chivalry. But Falstaff, in feigning death in battle, does not illustrate that "the better part of valour is discretion." Whereas Hal's challenge shows both valor and discretion because discretion is a function of reason, Falstaff's action shows neither: passion, not reason, controls his will.

True honor, then, can be achieved only by the exercise of full manhood; all the moral attributes must be kept in balance. Thus if action becomes a necessary moral obligation in a given situation inaction is labeled effeminacy. Warwick in *3 Henry VI*, when a battle is going badly, shouts

> I'll kill my horse, because I will not fly.
> Why stand we like soft-hearted women here.   (II. ii. 24–25)

Romeo, after Tybalt has wounded Mercutio, laments,

> O sweet Juliet,
> Thy beauty hath made me effeminate
> And in my temper soft'ned valour's steel!   (III. i. 118–120)

And at the end of *Richard II*, King Henry sarcastically says of Hal that

> he, young wanton and effeminate boy,
> Takes on the point of honour to support
> So dissolute a crew.   (V. iii. 10–12)

Hal's integrity is questioned because he bestows his attention on an unworthy object.

On the other hand, true honor is not merely an attribute bestowed by others. Bertram in *All's Well* defined honor as a familial attribute, but when he refuses to marry Helena because she is not nobly born, the King of France says of social honor: "the mere word's a slave." In his speech he gives the fullest definition of personal honor yet examined:

> From lowest place when virtuous things proceed,
> The place is dignified by th' doer's deed.
> Where great additions swell's, and virtue none,
> It is a dropsied honour . . .
> > She is young, wise, fair;
> In these to nature she's immediate heir;
> And these breed honour . . .
> > Honours thrive
> When rather from our acts we them derive
> Than our foregoers.   (II. iii. 132–144)

But the convincing logic of this statement is weakened when, after Bertram still refuses and Helena withdraws her request, the king shouts out, "My honour's at the stake." In Hamlet's eyes he proves himself rightly great, for he successfully binds the two in marriage if not through their mutual love, then through his determined anger!

To Hamlet, honor is "a fantasy and trick of fame" only when it is defined by the King of France's last usage of the word as reputation,[6] for Hamlet believes that true honor is the means to greatness:

> > Rightly to be great
> Is not to stir without great argument,
> But greatly to find quarrel in a straw
> When honour's at the stake.   (IV. iv. 53–56)

The context of this remark is especially important; Fortinbras' captain forthrightly has evaluated the objective of his army's mission as

> > a little patch of ground
> That hath in it no profit but the name.   (IV. iv. 18–19)

Hamlet reflects that not even "Two thousand souls and twenty thousand ducats" will settle this argument over a thing of no intrinsic worth. But Fortinbras has equated "the question of this straw" with the question of his personal integrity, and his activity serves as a mock to Hamlet's unaccomplished mission of revenge. Hamlet believes that he has "great argument"; hence, from the context of his remarks, he does not seek to gain honor as Fortinbras does. Acting upon "great argument" does not seem to Hamlet worthy of the addition of honor because fulfilling one's ethical duty is a moral obligation to one's human nature:

> What is a man,
> If his chief good and market of his time
> Be but to sleep and feed? A beast, no more.
> Sure he that made us with such large discourse,
> Looking before and after, gave us not
> That capability and godlike reason
> To fust in us unus'd.   (IV. iv. 33–39)

Yet, even though Hamlet would deny himself honor, we should recall that Brutus in *Julius Caesar* equates honor with "the general good" (I. ii. 85).

Thus the Shakespearean definitions of honor range from being nobly born to acting to correct social wrong. War alone is never romanticized, and its connection with honor is only incidental. By and large, honor applies to the qualities and actions of individual men, while war is a practical social concern.

THE THEATRICAL SETTING

This same distinction figures in the rival public and private plays of the period. For example, the very brief "Troilus and Cressida" of *Histrio-mastix* implies the conventional romantic attitude toward war as a proving ground in which honor is gained so that love then may be obtained; yet in the same play war is damned as the bringer of poverty and destroyer of peace and order (pp. 293–297). Between these poles there is a grand variety of attitudes toward honor and war.

When Guy, the nobly born of Heywood's four apprentices of London, finds respite at the court of France while on the way to the Holy Land, he tells a French lady that war is the glorious source of honor; in so doing he represents the extreme of heroic romance (pp. 180–181). Although Guy is unwavering before her tender enticements, he does not reject love entirely as does the hero of the anonymous *Captain Thomas Stukeley*, who prefers honor gained in battle to women, food, and money. In fact Stukeley's love of honor is so fixed that he abandons his bride and bankrupts his father-in-law so that he may pursue it. He is as cold as Tamburlaine where ethical ties are concerned; however, Mr. Curtis forgives all so long as honor is Stukeley's mark (ll. 775–776). Hermando de Medyna in the anonymous *The Weakest Goeth to the Wall* claims to be guided by the laws of knighthood (ll. 1468–1470), but he too believes that honor requires a Tamburlainian consistency in carrying out missions even if innocent children stand in his way (l. 576).

A more searching projection of honor as a positive good achieved in war is found in the person of Captain Bonvile in Heywood's *Royall King, and the Loyall Subject*. Having gained honor in the Holy Land, he pretends to be impoverished in order to see how far his reputation will maintain him in court circles. He finds all doors closed, and he is treated with the same contempt as is Jonson's Captain Tucca in *Poetaster*. Because Tucca is conceived in ridicule not respect it is not entirely clear how Jonson would have us react to Tucca's remark that "Honour's a good brooch to weare in a mans hat, at all times" (I. ii. 161–162). It is not even clear whether this is honor gained in war or a general attitude toward life.

The two conceptions are separate in Middleton's (?) *Blurt, Master-Constable* and the anonymous *Tryall of Chevalry*. On going to the wars Hippolito had sought honor, but upon return he admits to the mocking Violetta, "I am a new

man, sister, and now cry pox a' that honour that must have
none but barber-surgeons to wait upon't, and a band of poor
straggling rascals, that, every twinkling of an eye, forfeit
their legs and arms into the Lord's hands!" (I. i. 17–21).
Nonetheless, he feels that his sister has destroyed the family
honor by her conduct with Fontinelle, and he plots to
regain it (V. ii. 18–24). In the *Tryall*, while the Princes
Philip and Ferdinand proudly proclaim that their lives are
ruled by honor, they are quite willing to admit that "Force
cannot end this war, but policy." Their practical, but honorable approach even includes an entrapment and killing of
the villain Rodoricke which is much like Achilles' killing of
Hector: "Why had you thus ring'd me about with swords?"
(pp. 353, 346, 348). In contrast to Achilles' subsequent action, Sancto Danila in the anonymous *An Alarum for London* will not allow his soldiers to drag behind their horses
through Antwerp the bodies of Stump and the captain. Here
he is motivated by the "law of armes," and such an act, he
says, would disgrace the dead soldiers' honor (ll. 1639–
1658); but the "law of armes" did not prevent Danila at
the beginning of the play from employing deceit in order
to enter the city.

Whether the war should be governed by principle or expedience is ambiguous in Dekker's *Sir Thomas Wyatt*. Even
though Wyatt receives Norroy as a herald under "the lawe
of armes" and "the Arte of Warre," he smilingly implies that
those rules would not protect Norroy if Wyatt felt that his
death would help the insurgents (IV. i. 30–65). Bedford in
Day's *Blind Beggar of Bednal Green* follows the "Law of
Arms," but does not apply them to Momford, exiling rather
than killing him (sig. B₂). Momford, of course, is quite
concerned over the honor of his name, and stays disguised
in England in order to clear it.

The issue of moral responsibility for civil war and its toll is never brought to the surface in *Sir Thomas Wyatt*, each faction insisting on the correctness of its stand without much regard to consequences. The rapid pace of Heywood's *1* and *2 Edward IV* never allows for detailed commentary on the good and evil of war, although both aspects are mentioned. The theological question in Drayton's *1 Sir John Oldcastle* tends to cancel out the problem of rebellion; however, civil discord is clearly damned in the anonymous *Tryall of Chevalry*. Finally, war as the background of Marston's *Antonio and Mellida* is simply taken for granted, as it is in *Much Ado*.

Unfortunately, none of these plays shows a war being fought in an unworthy cause on the grounds of general honor. When Dekker's Sir Thomas Wyatt speaks of "this glorious quarrell" which will cause his followers to "stand in Chronicles ranck'd euen with Kings" (IV. i. 17–18) he sounds like Troilus in the council of Troy; but Wyatt's claim has a firm basis, for his cause is the protection of England from Spanish influence. The issues in *An Alarum for London* are such that English honor is only indirectly involved, but war is painted in all its destructive terror. On the other hand the play contains several examples of men acting on various principles of personal honor.

To Antonio in Marston's *Antonios Reuenge* the end of honor which will be reached by revenging his father's death justifies extreme means. This is clearly seen when he murders Julio, the son of Piero and his own mother:

> O that I knewe which joynt, which side, which lim,
> Were father all, and had no mother in't:
> That I might rip it vaine by vaine; and carve revenge
> In bleeding races: but since 'tis mixt together,
> Have at adventure, pel mell, no reverse.   (p. 103)

Marston rewards Antonio's adherence to purpose by indicating that his virtue will earn him a place in heaven and that he will live out his days on earth in peace and prayer. Hector had faced a similar problem when confronted by his cousin Ajax, but the ties of blood exercised a stronger demand on Hector than his desire for personal honor. In contradistinction to Antonio's action and in support of Hector's is the action of Phylander in the anonymous *Maydes Metamorphosis*; he decides not to kill Eurymine because

> A lawfull oath in an vnlawfull cause
> Is first dispenc't withall by reasons lawes.　　　(p. 108)

Hector's willful adherence to his oath to meet Achilles brought on his death. Lodowick in Chettle's *Hoffman* is as estimable as Hector, but opposite in nature; he is willing to forego a defense of Lucibella's honor in "tilt and turnameut" for a defense "by flight" (ll. 724–726). But Walt Terill in Dekker's *Satiromastix* seems to share Hector's respect for oaths, for he believes that he must carry out his pledge to his king even though it costs his bride her chastity. His honor is more important than hers. Caelestine sounds like Andromache and Cassandra when she asks,

> An oath? why, what's an oath? tis but the smoake,
> Of flame and bloud; the blister of the spirit,
> Which rizeth from the Steame of rage.

But his answer is equally strong and literally defines a concept of integrity.

> An oath? why tis the trafficke of the soule,
> Tis law within a man; the seale of faith,
> The bond of euery conscience.
> ·　·　·　·　·　·　·　·　·　·　·
> My oath is high, for to the King I swore.　　　(V. i. 32–50)

Even when Caelestine wishes to take poison as a "phisicke

against lust" so that she can preserve her honor and die a "true virgin" and "constant wife," Walter objects because her death would defeat his pledge and undermine his honor. Although her father, with Walter, never questions the king's right, he feels that Caelestine's death is necessary to preserve the several honors of all concerned. Only when he sarcastically asks, "What man would pledge a King in his owne wife?" do Walter's obligations to his wife finally overcome his concern for his oath and private honor (V. i. 130–162).

Dekker offers another study of the demands of love and honor in *The Shoemakers Holiday*, a particularly interesting study because it also involves the problems of war and of order. At the outset Lacy swears to his uncle that for the sake of honor he will

> So guide my actions in pursuit of *France*,
> As shall adde glorie to the *Lacies* name.

His uncle applauds and adds that where "Faire honour in her loftiest eminence" is waiting for a soldier, "shame attends delay" (I. i. 88–97).

It immediately becomes clear, however, that Lacy does not intend to go to France; indeed, he even lies again by telling his cousin that he will stay behind only three days. Lincoln later is shocked that his nephew has burned up his honor and credit "in the fire of . . . loues lunacie" (II. iv. 41), and Rose's father cannot understand how Lacy could "wrong his honor" by "Neglecting the hie charge the King imposed" (IV. iv. 5). By failing to fulfill his king's commission Lacy "Ranne himselfe deeply (in the highest degree) / Into vile treason" (V. v. 51–52). In fact, it is even implied that this absence from the field has caused a costly delay in prosecution of the war (V. v. 134–139). Still, in spite of this bill of indictment, the king not only forgives Lacy but knights him as well that he may regain his honor. The king's justification is simply that

> Twas not a base want of true valors fire,
> That kept him out of *France*, but loues desire.
>
> (V. v. 54–55)

The king is not neglectful of the war, nor does he take his kingship lightly; his closing words are about France and he refuses to exercise the power of the crown to divorce those whom God has joined together (V. v. 61–65). Along with its very real mirth, there is a moral seriousness in this play which might justify the taking of Lacy's example as a precedent in judging Achilles' withdrawal. And, finally, the war in France in general is a good, patriotic war, but when Jane is left alone, Rafe wounded, and she does not recognize his careworn face upon his return, we can agree that "these [be] bitter warres in *France*" (III. iv. 74).

CONCLUSION

Because Shakespeare's introduction of Hector's challenge and Ulysses' plan to meet the challenge are unique additions to the matter of Troy, the heroic manner in which he presented these plot elements is significant with regard to the themes of war and honor. Hector's challenge, nobly delivered by Aeneas, turns upon the concept of chivalric honor. Concerned for the honor of the Greek side, Ulysses delivers a moving admonition on the theme that "Perseverance, dear my lord, / Keeps honour bright" (III. iii. 150–151), even though he had said that he was going to use the "derision med'cinal" of comical satire in order to "physic" Achilles. Ajax, who was to have been the agent of Achilles' cure, enters this scene not as a ridiculous buffoon but as a noble warrior. Even when humbled by Hector, he admits he was wrong in seeking personal honor in his cousin's death. When his characterization here contradicts his earlier characterization as a vainglorious fool, we realize that Shakespeare could not forbear treating even Ajax with dignity in scenes of heroic display. Honor as defined in these particular cases is given positive endorsement when Shakespeare showed Hector visiting the Greek camp. Although visits to each other's camps were made by the rival forces in the medieval and Elizabethan versions of the Trojan war, Shakespeare did not turn Hector's visit into an empty, courtly show or a formal visit of state. Rather the dialogue is filled with a tone of veneration for the main persons of the siege story and of respect for the values which they represent — traditional "good matter" for the "common sort." Indeed, in this scene Shakespeare wrote in a manner which supports the claim made by Heywood in *An Apology for Actors* that the public theaters always portrayed Achilles, Hector, and Troilus as eminently noble and worthy.

In spite of these scenes, in the play as a whole chivalric honor is treated approvingly only to a degree. Although Troilus sounds the heroic note when he says that Helen

is a theme of honour and renown,
A spur to valiant and magnanimous deeds,   (II. ii. 199–200)

we know that he is wrong when he goes on to say that the war fought in her defense will "in time to come canonize us." The play seen in the light of its setting does not so much show contradictory attitudes toward war and honor as it suggests a usual distinction between honor as a moral attribute and war as an ethical concern. Shakespeare from *Henry VI* on down to *Troilus* never treated war in an attractive manner; he was even realistic in *Henry V* where he could have been merely jingoistic. Nevertheless, personal honor could always be gained in war, if it was incidental to the furthering of the general good. If the loss involved in war was too great or if the ethical motivation behind the war was unsound, then the quality of honor gained was clearly questioned.

These distinctions were also maintained in the rival plays of the day. Hippolito in Middleton's (?) *Blurt, Master-Constable*, is a brave man, but he clearly thinks that the price paid in soldiers' lives for honor in war is too high; however, the four brothers in Heywood's *The Four Prentises of London* gain honor in the Holy Land by fighting singlehandedly in a war which without reservation is known to be good. The limitation which the age seems to have placed on the quest for honor is most clearly and unconsciously present in plays such as *The Tryall of Chevalry* and *An Alarum for London*, where personal honor and integrity are maintained by fighting ill-justified wars in the most expeditious manner. If Shakespeare was in a mood to make these distinctions we can see why he chose the matter of Troy for his play.

Aerol Arnold has pointed out that the way in which Shakespeare develops the Hector-Andromache scene (V. iii) before the final battle indicates that he wished to emphasize that Hector's attitude toward personal honor is wrong.[7] Because only Shakespeare of all writers on the subject did not allow Andromache, Cassandra, and Priam to dissuade Hector from fighting, we may assume that he wished to show that Hector is not justified in ignoring his obligations to the bonds of marriage and the ties of blood merely because he "Holds honour far more precious-dear than life" (V. ii. 28). But, as Hector is with Troilus, so we are with him: although we can say that he is wrong, it is hard to condemn him.

Thus, once having chosen the matter of Troy Shakespeare followed his own precedent, the theatrical practice of his day, and his sources in showing that honor is a positive value if it is sought with due regard for ethical considerations. If kept harmlessly on a man-to-man basis, or sought within ethically justified strife, honor is a worthy attribute. But this latter case could be illustrated only negatively when one used the Troy material. Hector justifiably may challenge a Greek to single combat; however, he is wrong when he endorses Troilus' position that personal honor may be gained in defending Helen: he knows that the war is being waged in a worthless cause.[8]

CHAPTER VII · THE RHETORIC
OF ORDER AND DISORDER

*A*GAMEMNON opens the Greek plot by revealing in a council scene (I. iii) which precedes
but parallels the Trojan council that the Greek
princes have shown discontent because "after seven years'
siege yet Troy walls stand." He tries to allay their dis-
appointment by stating in terms which echo Vergil both
in latinate diction and in long epic similes what to Shakespeare would have been the pagan, Roman philosophy of
Stoicism. The whole speech is in perfect decorum: aloof,
learned, and signifies very little. There follows another in
perfect decorum when Nestor the old warrior and statesman
restates the question in flowing senatorial tone and terms.
All is rant so far — but rant majestically phrased, classically
embroidered, and platitudinously philosophic. Now Ulysses
steps forward. His opening words in address to the General
and Nestor are in the formal, social manner that one would
associate with the traditional "politic" Ulysses. The compli-
ments are stiff and long, and the sixteen lines ask only for
permission to speak. Agamemnon consents and Ulysses begins his speech on "Order." This speech, too, is latinate, at
least in comparison to Shakespeare's more normal diction.[1]
However, it is charged with ideas, has the forward press of
active thought, and absorbs our attention.[2] There is little
posturing, and the facile stoicism of Agamemnon is replaced
with a positive conception of moral, ethical, and world
order.[3] The immediate burden is that

> The specialty of rule hath been neglected;
> And look, how many Grecian tents do stand
> Hollow upon this plain, so many hollow factions.

(I. iii. 78–80)

Although Ulysses goes on in a generalized manner to discourse on the philosophic necessity for degree and order in any microcosm of the great macrocosm, he begins and ends with the implication that it is Agamemnon who is responsible for all the Greek disorder and inaction. But the King never draws the appropriate inference, the Greeks continue in confusion, and success comes only with the almost accidental death of Hector, the last hope of Troy. Certainly Ulysses' elevated, philosophical rhetoric does not exercise control on the outcome.

Counterpointing Ulysses' great speeches is the low invective of Thersites remarkable for its imagery of digestion and disease. Thersites ought to be dismissed as a kind of "allowed fool" because of his traditional rhetorical function as railer, but he is so completely and believably drawn that, as Kenneth Muir accurately observes, "however much we discount Thersites' railings, some of the mud he throws is bound to stick." [4] Indeed, it ought to have been unnecessary, but H. B. Charlton was forced to note that Achilles' "homosexuality [is] nothing but the report of a known slanderer." [5] Even "objective" textual criticism of the play has been seduced by the power of Thersites' rhetoric into finding more decadence than the text warrants, scholars insisting, to give a small example, that Patroclus be called Achilles "brach" (II. i. 126) instead of his "brooch." [6] On a larger scale the voice of Thersites has led George W. Meyer to believe that the play is a "panorama of military disorder and sexual depravity, a dramatic *pousse-café* made up of married and unmarried, male and female, heterosexual, bisexual, and homosexual Greeks and Trojans." [7]

THE PROBLEM OF THE GREEK PLOT

The full picture of the disorder in the Greek camp and the main thematic concern of the Greek plot are vividly presented in Ulysses' first long speech. But the burden is the simple implication that Agamemnon has not commanded; and as a result,

> When that the general is not like the hive,
> To whom the foragers shall all repair,
> What honey is expected?
>
> .   .   .   .
>
>   The general's disdain'd
> By him one step below, he by the next;
> That next by him beneath. So every step,
> Exampled by the first pace that is sick
> Of his superior, grows to an envious fever
> Of pale and bloodless emulation. (I. iii. 83–85, 129–134)

As Nestor and Agamemnon are quick to point out, Ulysses has exposed "The nature of the sickness," martial weakness and personal emulation; that Ulysses' speech has been, in a way, an example itself of the kind of thing it describes is missed by Agamemnon, for he asks, "What is the remedy?" The remedy has been implied already and Ulysses can hardly afford to assert it openly. Rather, he continues his indirection, describing the "envious fever" in the Greek camp:

> The great Achilles, whom opinion crowns
> The sinew and the forehand of our host,
> Having his ear full of his airy fame,
> Grows dainty of his worth and in his tent
> Lies mocking our designs. (I. iii. 142–146)

Although the indictment against Achilles is detailed and damaging, Ulysses' main concern is still the specialty of rule; Agamemnon must reassert his authority. Gladys D. Willcock has suggested, indeed, that when he shows how Achilles has Patroclus mimic Agamemnon, Ulysses "by a

ruthless sharpening of the rhetorical weapon which Putten-
ham christened the 'fleering frumpe' . . . applies the goad
to affronted egotism." [8] But Agamemnon misses the point.
Thus after Nestor points out that Ajax and Thersites — "A
slave whose gall coins slanders like a mint" — are in emulous
imitation of the first pair, Ulysses can only conclude in summary that the action of all four shows that they respect acts
"of hand" not of "wisdom"; to them the innate battering
is more important than

> those that with the fineness of their souls
> By reason guide his execution.   (I. iii. 209–210)

As was the case with Pandarus, certain of the Greeks treat
the positive, moral qualities of traditional humanism in a
light manner.

Ulysses still has not stated the remedy which Agamemnon
requested; nevertheless, he has clearly illustrated that the
Greek cause is on the brink of chaos. If he has a remedy in
mind other than the veiled suggestion that Agamemnon
should assert himself, we do not find out because a trumpet
sounds from the direction of Troy and the entrance of
Aeneas ends the council. When Aeneas asks as "a herald
and a prince" if he may give a message to Agamemnon in
person, the king answers:

> With surety stronger than Achilles' arm
> Fore all the Greekish heads, which with one voice
> Call Agamemnon head and general.   (I. iii. 220–222)

Of course, the Greeks would never show a hand of weakness
to the Trojans, but the audience has just seen that the "Greek
heads" do not "with one voice" acknowledge Agamemnon
as leader. That Agamemnon does not realize the importance
of Ulysses' diagnosis is ironically proved. As in the Trojan
council scene, all the magnificent philosophic rhetoric has

been in vain with regard to plot, and this scene also ends with the challenge as the topic.

The challenge gives Ulysses the opening he needs to get Achilles back into action, but he acts by ruse not so much because he is sly as because Agamemnon has not been able to see what he must do. The action proper leading up to the trial by arms is rather dull: the plotting of Ulysses and Nestor, the special pleading before Achilles, the baiting of Ajax, and the ranting of Thersites. If anyone should doubt the efficiency of such labels for Thersites as *caustic, bitter, vile, diseased*, let him but read aloud the opening speeches of Act II. We have not colloquy so much as cacophony:

> *Ajax*. Thersites!
> *Thersites*. Agamemnon — how if he had biles — full, all over, generally?
> *Ajax*. Thersites!
> *Thersites*. And those biles did run — say so? Did not the general run then? Were not that a botchy core?
> *Ajax*. Dog!
> *Thersites*. Then would come some matter from him. I see none now.
> *Ajax*. Thou bitch-wolf's son, canst thou not hear? Feel then.
> . . . .
> *Thersites*. Dost thou think I have no sense, thou strik'st me thus? (II. i. 1–24)

But what emerges in a serious vein is the character of Achilles. Up until the end of II. i, which serves mainly to introduce Thersites, Ajax, Patroclus, and Achilles, Achilles shows only that he is somewhat amused by all the present bickering. But now he begins to reveal more of himself as he tells Ajax about the challenge. He is troubled as he breaks off his relation when he gets to the part about each combatant's willingness to maintain his lady "wiser, fairer, truer." He says that the challenger must be

> such a one that dare
> Maintain — I know not what. 'Tis trash. Farewell.

(II. i. 137–138)

He leaves in frustration, for, as the audience well knew, he has pledged Hecuba that out of proof of his love for Polyxena he will no longer fight the Trojans.[9]

Scholars have noted that Peele, like Shakespeare, has Achilles fall in love with Polyxena before Hector's death, whereas Caxton, Lydgate, and the other medieval sources had reversed the order. What has not been noted is that Greene's *Euphues*, I. O.'s *The Lamentation of Troy for the Death of Hector* (1594), and the Admiral's plot fragment also show that Achilles fell in love with Priam's daughter before he killed Hector. Hence it would seem that in this case Shakespeare did not change the Troy material but followed an "Elizabethan" version of why Achilles withdrew from battle early in the war. When we recall that Homer began to come into prominence again during the sixteenth century, this departure from Caxton can be understood as a transitional confusion of Achilles' love of Briseis at the beginning of the *Iliad* and his love of Polyxena toward the end of Caxton's account of the ten years' war. Recognition of an Elizabethan belief on this point is important because our sophisticated insight into Homer's glorification of Achilles' pride for its own sake would have made little sense to Shakespeare. In the next scene (II. iii), the embassy to Achilles, after Patroclus has said that Achilles is "ill-dispos'd," and Ulysses has answered that the counsellors know that he is not sick, Ajax responds, "Yes, lion-sick, sick of proud heart. You may call it melancholy, if you will favour the man; but, by my head, 'tis pride. But why, why? Let him show us a cause" (93–96). Even Ajax knows that every effect must have a cause; Achilles may be full of pride, but the reason for his elevation of personal concern over the general welfare is that he, like Troilus and Paris, is a victim of love.

When Patroclus returns a second time to say that Achilles will not see his visitors, Agamemnon's angered speech in rebuttal affirms once more the idea that virtue is not merely a singular achievement:

> all his virtues,
> Not virtuously on his own part beheld,
> Do in our eyes begin to lose their gloss;
> Yea, like fair fruit in an unwholesome dish,
> Are like to rot untasted.   (II. iii. 126–130)

And the simile, like so many others, contributes to an objective quality in the play, an effect of distancing, so that it is not "we" but "they" and only they to whom things are happening. As Agamemnon continues, his words recall the thematic concern of the Greek plot along with their direct criticism of Achilles:

> you shall not sin
> If you do say we think him over-proud
> And under-honest, in self-assumption greater
> Than in the note of judgment; and worthier than himself
> Here tend the savage strangeness he puts on,
> Disguise the holy strength of their command,
> And underwrite in an observing kind
> His humorous predominance.   (II. iii. 131–138)

In the next scene in the Greek camp (III. iii) Ulysses seems to have found the means of counteracting Achilles' "humorous predominance" when he asks all the leaders to pass by Achilles "As if he were forgot," because

> I have derision med'cinable
> To use between your strangeness and his pride,
> Which his own will shall have desire to drink.

It may do good. Pride hath no other glass
To show itself but pride; for supple knees
Feed arrogance and are the proud man's fees.

> (III. iii. 44–49)

In I. iii, Ulysses and Nestor decided to "physic the great
Myrmidon" by pronouncing Ajax "as the worthier man."
Now, in order to set a philosophical tone for his praise of
Ajax and his derision of Achilles, Ulysses follows the rest
pretending to be deeply engrossed in a book, the thesis of
which is that virtue is not a particular or singular quality,
rather it is twofold: it both resides in the man and is attrib-
uted to him by others. This idea is a corollary to the one
stated by Hector in Ilium and has been mentioned by
Aeneas and Agamemnon; Pandarus even had incorporated
it in his banter with Cressida, and Achilles is quick to agree
to the position because he has touched upon the thought just
now (76–78) as he watched the leaders go by. Thus Ulysses
is able to prepare the way for his derision by saying that
Ajax is "unknown" because he does not know his own great
virtues nor are they fully realized by the camp. But when
the Greeks applaud his victory over Hector on the morrow
Ajax will be "renowned," and all because fortune cast the
lot in his direction. Achilles takes the bait:

I do believe it; for they pass'd by me
As misers do by beggars; neither gave to me
Good word nor look. What, are my deeds forgot?

> (III. iii. 142–144)

This touching befuddlement, honest and open, introduces
one of the finest arias in Shakespeare, "Time hath, my lord,
a wallet at his back." The speech says beautifully and movingly that because man in his fallen nature does not see life
steadily and see it whole, absolute judgment becomes relative
judgment; as a result he who would claim the addition of

greatness must be ever ready to defend that title against all challengers. In sum, because,

> One touch of nature makes the whole world kin,
>
> .   .   .   .
>
> The present eye praises the present object.
> Then marvel not, thou great and complete man,
> That all the Greeks begin to worship Ajax,
> Since things in motion sooner catch the eye
> Than what not stirs. The cry went once on thee,
> And still it might, and yet it may again,
> If thou wouldst not entomb thyself alive
> And case thy reputation in thy tent.   (III. iii. 175–187)

When Achilles remains unmoved, Ulysses goes on to reveal bluntly the plain truth that Achilles' love for Polyxena has been discovered, and makes his final appeal to Achilles' pride by presenting an argument that would apply to Hector: affairs of state and obligations to family are "reasons . . . more potent and heroical" than any private and particular reasons which Achilles can offer in justification of his inactivity. At this point he becomes derisive for the first time:

> All the commerce that you have had with Troy
> As perfectly is ours as yours, my lord;
> And better would it fit Achilles much
> To throw down Hector than Polyxena.   (III. iii. 205–208)

Nevertheless, Ulysses has tried to be persuasive rather than derisive; his medicine has been gentle and ministering to the mind. We believe him when he says,

> Farewell, my lord. I as your lover speak.
> The fool slides o'er the ice that you should break.
>
>   (III. iii. 213–214)

Ulysses is not the first to suggest that Achilles' love of

Polyxena is unworthy, for Patroclus reminds Achilles that he too has tried to move him "To this effect." Because of the unwarranted but widely assumed homosexual attachment of these two, the serious import of Patroclus' speeches at this point can be overlooked all too easily. We must remember that the only accusation of homosexuality in the play is made by the known slanderer Thersites, and even he says that Patroclus will give anything for "a commodious drab." Furthermore, Patroclus talks about Polyxena not jealously as if she were a rival, but sincerely, out of respect for Achilles. And when he speaks of "your great love to me" and calls Achilles "sweet," he is using the accepted language of male friendship; indeed the language of polite intercourse: Troilus so addresses Ulysses, and Ulysses, Achilles. Finally, Renaissance rhetoric books cited Achilles and Patroclus among the traditional pairs of friends.

The dialogue continues to move quite seriously, and Achilles seems on the point of being persuaded:

My mind is troubled like a fountain stirr'd;
And I myself see not the bottom of it.   (III. iii. 310–311)

The implication of "Know Thyself" and the serious personal agony of a man's being drawn by the opposing forces of love and honor are undercut, however, by the purposeless execration of the lowly Thersites which ends the scene: "Would the fountain of your mind were clear again, that I might water an ass at it! I had rather be a tick in a sheep than such a valiant ignorance."

The war for Achilles' soul exercised by public and private demands continues through the rest of the play, but in a way which does not emphasize the pull of opposite forces. Achilles decides to fight again after the trial by combat because he is taunted into it by Hector and the "new" Ajax, not out of patriotic duty. Then his mind is changed by a letter from Hecuba and Polyxena, not by conscience. And the death of Patroclus brings him into the final battle, not the fact that the battle is going against the Greeks, and that, as a result, "the Grecians began to proclaim barbarism, and policy grows into an ill opinion" (V. iv. 17–18). The words are Thersites' and in spite of the danger of taking whatever he says at face value, it is hard not to agree:

> Take but degree away . . .
> And appetite, an universal wolf . . .
> Must make perforce an universal prey.

The last chaotic scene of the play mirrors well the discord and strife that mark the resolution of each plot-line, especially the accidental success of the Greeks, and provides the perfect context for the shrill voice of Thersites. For example, when Menelaus and Paris enter in a skirmish, the emblematic value of their fight is obvious; nevertheless, Thersites emphasizes it: "The cuckold and the cuckold-maker are at it. Now, bull! now, dog! 'Loo, Paris, 'loo! Now my double-henn'd sparrow! 'Loo, Paris, 'loo! The bull has the game. Ware horns, ho!" (V. vii. 9–13). But Thersites has had his day, and now is dismissed in a most ignominious way. He is made to confess to bastardy and cowardice: "I am bastard begot, bastard instructed, bastard in mind, bastard in valor, in everything illegitimate"; he runs out never to be heard from again.

After Hector's death — an ugly, planned murder, not a fateful culmination of a matched encounter — Achilles compounds his brutality with dishonesty and callousness:

> On, Myrmidons, and cry you amain,
> 'Achilles hath the mighty Hector slain.'
>
> .   .   .   .
>
> Come, tie his body to my horse's tail;
> Along the field I will the Troyan trail.   (V. viii. 13–22)

When Diomedes announces that "Hector's slain, and by Achilles," Agamemnon reveals that Ulysses' diagnosis of the cause of the Grecian troubles has never affected him; the Greeks muddled through to success, though without having solved their basic problem:

> Let one be sent
> To pray Achilles see us at our tent.
> If in his [Hector's] death the gods have us befriended,
> Great Troy is ours, and our sharp wars are ended.
>
> (V. ix. 7–10)

The problem that arises out of the Greek plot is, then, why is so much elevated rhetoric devoted to the theory of the microcosm-macrocosm and to the obligations of leadership and public duty only to see all undercut by both petty and selfish actions, all of which is counterpointed by the debased rhetoric of Thersites?

THE SHAKESPEAREAN PRECEDENT

It is needless to belabor the point that Shakespeare's plays are filled with long, learned speeches, but a hasty review of the quality and quantity of these speeches in general as they lead to those in *Troilus and Cressida* may better explain the awkward relationship of the rhetoric of Hector and Ulysses to plot-lines and themes. All the main characters in *2 Henry VI* have at least one lengthy, rhetorical declamation, which must have made the play an actor's favorite. But these speeches, probably Shakespeare's first, are an extreme example of what Virgil Whitaker has demonstrated in *Shakespeare's Use of Learning*: learning and rhetoric do not always subserve the dramatic necessities of action, character, and theme in the very early plays. The learning in *Richard III*, *The Comedy of Errors*, *The Two Gentlemen of Verona*, *Love's Labour's Lost*, and *Titus Andronicus* is sometimes "bookish" and seemingly presented for its own sake, and the rhetoric can be noticeably stylized. These two qualities, though, are utilized with special advantage in *Richard II* where Richard's speeches are filled, for example, with king-sun-God imagery drawn from the Elizabethan view of the world and a love of rhetorical display is an essential part of his character. Thus decorum is maintained while the play is given the necessary microcosmic-macrocosmic background out of which its thematic motifs develop.

Friar Laurence's speeches are not merely gratuitous entertainment but supply the moral and ethical philosophy by which the love of Romeo and Juliet is evaluated. Because he is old, if he is tedious, at least the tediousness fits his character. But Portia's speech on "the quality of mercy" stands out of context too prominently, even though it supplies a necessary theme for *The Merchant of Venice*. On the other hand, the constant and consistent delight of *The Taming of the Shrew* could have been its sufficient justification; even so, the play points a moral:

> Such duty as the subject owes the prince,
> Even such a woman oweth to her husband.   (V. ii. 155–156)

We know from Ulysses' speech and the Elizabethan habit of mind that this analogy is not mere decoration. As the "new" Katharina goes on, a concept of world order is assumed:

> I am asham'd that women are so simple
> To offer war where they should kneel for peace;
> Or seek for rule, supremacy, and sway
> When they are bound to serve, love, and obey.
>   (V. ii. 161–164)

We have noted that what gives *Venus and Adonis* a complex final tone is Venus' light attitude toward love played against Adonis' serious moral philosophy, and we saw also that philosophic motifs are introduced and developed throughout *Lucrece*. If from our point of view Lucrece is boring in her apostrophes on Time, Opportunity, and Night, certainly she is not in her lengthy attempt to dissuade Tarquin from his lecherous intent. Although she does not focus on herself, but reminds Tarquin of his moral and ethical obligations as a man and as a ruler, Shakespeare so infused his poetry with powerful emotion that she is never in danger of appearing merely high-minded. Her last appeal combines in metaphor her two main lines of defense:

> To thee, to thee, my heav'd-up hands appeal,
> Not to seducing lust, thy rash relier!
> I sue for exil'd majesty's repeal;
> Let him return, and flatt'ring thoughts retire.
> His true respect will prison false desire
>   And wipe the dim mist from thy doting eyne,
>   That thou shalt see thy state, and pity mine.   (ll. 638–644)

And her innocent question before the painting of the fall of Troy,

> Why should the private pleasure of some one
> Become the public plague of many moe?   (ll. 1478–1479)

is the one raised by *Hamlet*, dramatized in *Troilus*, and answered in *Lear*.

Such a question would be meaningless and lead to pessimism if the kind of philosophy detailed and summarized in Richard Hooker's *Laws of Ecclesiastical Polity* and Sir John Davies' *Nosce Teipsum* did not lie behind it, charging the question with emotional and cerebral significance. Indeed, what unifies the sonnet sequence of Shakespeare is not a story with several ambiguous twists in it; it is the accumulative statement of Christian humanism that evolves out of the total experience of all the poems.

What vitalizes their conventional forms is the feeling of a mind working through and ordering experience; as a result, the separate sonnets afford insights into the conflicting demands of flesh and spirit, passion and reason, private life and public life, life here and hereafter, and all the various interlocking dualisms of Renaissance thought and faith which were known to affect the life of man. As a total expression they are a wise affirmation of an hierarchical view of reality and value which gives meaning and purpose to life. The assumptions of felt belief in "When, in disgrace with Fortune and men's eyes" (Sonnet 29), for example, are so entire and positive that the poem can be read as either a love poem or a meditation on things divine; no awkward ambiguities or wrenching ambivalences are necessary to account for this twofold reading simply because the humanist spirit of Elizabethan England embraced both heaven and earth.

This reminder concerning Shakesperean thought is necessary in order to help us see the long, learned speeches in the serious plays of 1598 to 1603 in a larger context. The comedies of this period are generally conceived with a primary emphasis on situation and character. Jaques halts the pace of *As You Like It* with his mildly satiric and pessimistic disquisition on the life of man, and lengthy ethical reflections, light as well as serious, abound in *All's Well*; even so, the comedies of this period do not have the bookish, learned decoration for its own sake of the earliest ones.

Henry V, *Julius Caesar*, and *Hamlet* illustrate successively how well Shakespeare brought his learning into mesh with the over-all decorum of a play. The opening scenes of *Henry V* would seem to give the lie to this generalization because the speeches of the Archbishop of Canterbury on the Salique Law and on the necessity for obedience within the "state of man" which provide the philosophical frame of the play seem to be ignored by the king. Even though Henry does not seem to have paid much attention to the justification of his claim to the throne of France or to the long *exemplum* of the honeybees,

> Creatures that by a rule in nature teach
> The act of order to a peopled kingdom,   (I. ii. 188–189)

he is sufficiently convinced that he is King of France "by gift of heaven, / By law of nature and of nations" (II. iv. 79–80) to invade the continent. Once on the continent Henry begins to weave the previously introduced philosophy into his own speeches. As a result his meditation on the "hard condition" of kingship is more than an outburst of personal doubt and weariness: it raises universal questions concerning "place, degree, and form" (IV. i. 263).

From the very beginning of *Julius Caesar* the speeches of Cassius and Brutus and Antony are filled with the psychological and philosophical elements which give meaning to the theme of "Domestic fury and fierce civil strife" which follow the murder of a ruler. Brutus well summarizes the nature of his own precarious position with regard to Cassius' temptation:

> Between the acting of a dreadful thing
> And the first motion, all the interim is
> Like a phantasma or a hideous dream.
> The genius and the mortal instruments
> Are then in council, and the state of man,
> Like to a little kingdom, suffers then
> The nature of an insurrection.   (II. i. 63–69)

And Antony hyperbolically comments on the consequences of the decision which Brutus finally made:

> O judgment, thou art fled to brutish beasts,
> And men have lost their reason!   (III. ii. 110–111)

The humanistic emphasis on the need for order in man, the state, and universe is further developed in *Hamlet*. Indeed, Theodore Spencer in *Shakespeare and the Nature of Man* has pointed out that not a single long speech by Hamlet fails to touch upon the philosophical relationship of the microcosm to the macrocosm. Hamlet's famous apostrophe on the glories of the universe and man (II. ii) is an open statement of the kind of thought that permeates the play. We saw in the last chapter how it enters "How all occasions do inform against me," but it appears even in Hamlet's first soliloquy. Pondering his mother's hasty marriage, he exclaims:

> O God! a beast that wants discourse of reason
> Would have mourn'd longer.   (I. ii. 150–151)

Hamlet compounds with the idea of sovereign reason's overthrow an equal emphasis on the resultant dominance of lust's force. His father's ghost expresses well this double concern:

> But virtue, as it never will be mov'd,
> Though lewdness court it in a shape of heaven,
> So lust, though to a radiant angel link'd,
> Will sate itself in a celestial bed
> And prey on garbage.   (I. v. 53–57)

That "reason panders will" is a mild phrasing of this twin motif which Hamlet develops at length in the closet scene. His assumptions are clearly stated; his mother is old enough to start being wise:

> You cannot call it love; for at your age
> The heyday in the blood is tame, it's humble,
> And waits upon the judgment.   (III. iv. 68–70)

Even if she claims a sensual inclination toward Claudius, he believes that

> sense to ecstasy was ne'er so thrall'd
> But it reserv'd some quantity of choice.   (III. iv. 74–75)

Because he does not question the truth of these principles, his frustrated ire turns into a chastising raillery:

> Nay, but to live
> In the rank sweat of an enseamed bed,
> Stew'd in corruption, honeying and making love
> Over the nasty sty!   (III. iv. 91–94)

This kind of diction continues even after Gertrude has put herself under Hamlet's sway, so that his highly sensuous description of how to repulse the advances of Claudius in order that custom and use may begin to work toward easy abstinence is almost prurient (III. iv. 181–196). Although Hamlet asks forgiveness for his coarseness, he offers a Juvenalian justification: it is a "virtue" which he must exercise "in the fatness of these pursy times" (152–155). Imagery of disease, thanks to Thersites, abounds in *Troilus and Cressida*. But Caroline Spurgeon has pointed out that *Hamlet*, mainly because of the hero's nauseated reaction to his mother's lust, has twice the amount that is in *Troilus* and is second only to *Troilus* in imagery of food and digestion.[10] Thersites may be unique in the canon, but recognition that other characters in Shakespeare, even Hamlet, are blunt in speech and "forceful" in their selection of diction may tend to make Thersites appear less strange.

The Lieutenant in *2 Henry VI* does not hedge in his evaluation of Suffolk:

> Pool? Sir Pool? Lord!
> Ay, kennel, puddle, sink! whose filth and dirt
> Troubles the silver spring where England drinks.
>   (IV. i. 70–72)

The Duke of York in *3 Henry VI* calls Margaret a "She-

wolf" and "an Amazonian trull" who has a "tiger's heart
wrapp'd in a woman's hide" (I. iv. 137). Margaret's curse
of his son Richard shows that she too is well schooled in
vitriolic diction:

> thou art neither like thy sire nor dam,
> But like a foul misshapen stigmatic,
> Mark'd by the Destinies to be avoided,
> As venom toads or lizards' dreadful stings.   (II. ii. 135–138)

But sweet Lady Anne in *Richard III* over the corpse of
Henry VI and in direct address to Richard puts the queen
to shame — that is, until Margaret herself enters in the next
scene and vents her rage at great length upon the "poisonous
bunch-back'd toad" (I. iii. 246). The general abuse in *Titus
Andronicus* is richly phrased, as is the specific abuse of Shy-
lock in *The Merchant of Venice*. But diction alone does not
wholly account for the repulsiveness of Thersites. If he instead of Pistol had said,

> Yoke-fellows in arms,
> Let us to France, like horse-leeches, my boys,
> To suck, to suck, the very blood to suck!
>
> (II. iii. 56–58)

we would not smile.

All the plays of 1598–1603 except for *Henry V* have one
character who is in some degree a melancholic malcontent.[11]
It is within the context of this character type as well as in the
context of diction that Thersites is to be understood. The
bastard Don John, the "plain-dealing villain" of *Much Ado*,
is the first of these Saturnine persons, and the most experimental. Jaques is the "Monsieur Melancholy" of *As You
Like It* (III. ii. 312), but unlike the Don he merely rails and
does not seek active revenge:

> Give me leave
> To speak my mind, and I will through and through

Cleanse the foul body of th' infected world,
If they will patiently receive my medicine. (II. vii. 58–61)

Jaques has been a traveler and thinks that he has gained through experience the wisdom necessary to correct the follies of the world, but the good Duke Senior thinks otherwise:

> all th' embossed sores and headed evils
> That thou with license of free foot has caught,
> Wouldst thou disgorge into the general world.
>
> (II. vii. 67–69)

In retort Jaques hides behind the Horatian claim that it is the vice and not the man that he attacks.

Malvolio, the discontented wisher-of-ill in *Twelfth Night*, is brought into the structure more effectively than the previous two. Yet he is kin to them and is judged by standards which oppose his own. In addition to Sir Toby's famous rebuke there is the more balanced and authoritative one of Oliva: "O, you are sick of self-love, Malvolio, and taste with a distemper'd appetite. To be generous, guiltless, and of free disposition, is to take those things for birdbolts that you deem cannon bullets. There is no slander in an allow'd fool, though he do nothing but rail; nor no railing in a known discreet man, though he do nothing but reprove" (I. v. 97–104). Malvolio and his kind mistake partial truth for whole truth and illusion for reality, as is so comically proved in this play.

The line of descent from the bastard Don John to Thersites may seem at first hardly continuous; however, if we think of Parolles as coming between Thersites and Jaques, the kinship of these Shakespearean malcontents can be seen. Like Thersites, Parolles is a soldier of undetermined but sufficiently high rank to be a hanger-on of the officers and gentry. Like Jaques, he claims to have been a traveler and hence feels that he is in a position to comment upon men, manners, and customs. But when upon first entering the play he mocks the laws of nature and the principle of rational increase as detailed by Hooker, we do not have to wait long to be convinced that he is "a notorious liar . . . a great way fool, solely a coward" (I. i. 111–112).

Hamlet, too, confesses to melancholy and discontent, and there is no reason that we should not believe him. Even though Shakespeare has created a character in Hamlet that cannot be fitted into any one mold, perhaps we are safe in attributing Hamlet's excessively suggestive outbursts against lust to the psychological malaise that leads to abusive raillery.[12] It is an odious comparison, but there is a touch of consanguinity between Hamlet and Thersites.

THE THEATRICAL SETTING

The speeches of Hector and Ulysses in their respective councils and Ulysses' addressing Achilles are like other "philosophical lyrics" in Shakespeare which are created out of the Renaissance commonplaces concerning the inherent dignity and apparent frailty of man, conceived in another world but born into this one, constantly striving to maintain order in all his "worlds," small and large, so that life may have joy and meaning. And man, his condition in the world, and the powers of the universe likewise afford the burdens for many meditations and apostrophes in the rival plays of the period, most of which contain satiric observers of the human comedy as well.

While musing over the activities of his son, Lorenzo, Sr., in the first version of Jonson's *Every Man in his Humour*, delivers a speech that is interesting for two reasons: first, it is quite typical in style and content of many other speeches which are couched in the learning of the day; and, second, Jonson changed it completely sometime before 1616. The

way in which the speech opens reveals how it really will
range far beyond the particular question at hand:

> My labouring spirit being late opprest
> With my sonnes follie, can embrace no rest,
> Till it hath plotted by aduise and skill,
> How to reduce him from affected will
> To reasons manage; which while I intend,
> My troubled soule beginnes to apprehend
> A farther secret, and to meditate
> Vpon the difference of mans estate:
> Where is deciphered to true iudgements eye
> A deep, conceald, and precious misterie.   (II. ii. 1–10)

The speech goes on abstracting and generalizing about how
"natures art" created "Reason (as a king)" in the body,
moves into familial, social, and political analogies, and ends
awkwardly by reverting to the fact that "my sonne haue
done him [Lord Reason] too much wrong" (II. ii. 17–36).
Because its diction is abstract, the speech has a learned tone.
When Jonson's revision proves to be a Timon-like diatribe
against the fashionable, modern world, perhaps it is not so
much a sign that Jonson's interest turned to satire after
1598 as that, by 1616, the original kind of speech was out of
style.

We have seen how the king in *The Shoemakers Holiday*
referred to the order of nature under God; the opening
scene of Heywood's *Royall King, and the Loyall Subject*
reveals a similar concern. The king firmly asserts that order
must be re-established now that the holy wars are over, and
he is aware that the responsibility is his; he must exercise his
"prerogative" of rule and bring to bear on the kingship all
"my operant parts" (pp. 5–8). Dekker's *Sir Thomas Wyatt*
likewise firmly believes that order must be maintained in
the realm through adherence to the political hierarchy or-

dained by God. When Arundel seeks to crown Lady Jane
Grey in order to avoid the immediate problems which would
come with the succession of Catholic Mary, Wyatt will allow
no relativistic, pragmatic solution:

> In actions roauing from the bent of truth,
> We haue no persident thus to persist
> But the bare name of worldly policie.
> If others haue ground from Iustice, and the law,
> As well diuine as politicke agreeing,
> They are for no cause to be disinherited.
>
> .   .   .   .
>
>   Be strong and bold:
> We are the peoples factors. Saue our Sonnes
> From killing one another, be affraide,
> To tempt both heauen and earth, so I haue said.
>
>   (I. vi. 66–99)

Hubert, King John's minion in Munday's *Death of Robert,
Earl of Huntington*, strongly opposes and criticizes his
king's lust, but he fully accepts his obligation to obey the
king's authority (pp. 300–301). Chrisoganus in Marston's
Histrio-mastix uses the "body politic" metaphor to describe
the need for law and order in a nation; he concludes,

>   if the arme make warre against the head,
> Or that the heart rebell against the braine,
> This elementall bodie (thus compact,)
> Is but a scattred *Chaos* of revenge;
> Your lawes appoincted to be positive,
> (By *Warre* confounded) must be brought againe.
> For law is that which Love and Peace maintaine.   (p. 296)

And Andrugio, the exiled Duke in Marston's *Antonio and
Mellida*, gives a similar type of speech, but one reversing
the point of view; he looks on the laws of the world in a
manner which is just the opposite of Hooker's:

My thoughts are fixt in contemplation
Why this huge earth, this monstrous animal,
That eats her children, should not have eyes & ears.
Philosophie maintaines that Natur's wise,
And formes no uselesse or unperfect thing.
Did Nature make the earth, or the earth Nature?
For earthly durt makes all things, makes the man,
Moulds me up honour; and like a cunning Dutchman,
Paints me a puppit even with seeming breath,
And gives a sot appearance of a soule.
Goe to, goe to; thou liest, Philosophy.
Nature formes things unperfect, uselesse, vaine. (pp. 31–32)

This is not a parody, but speeches on order were so common that parodies provided an easy source of laughter. Middleton's Dryfat seems to assume the stance and theme of Ulysses when, disguised as a proctor, he says that if the Family of Love is not suppressed, "each man's copyhold will become freehold, specialties will turn to generalities, and so from unity to parity, from parity to plurality, and from plurality to universality; their wives, the only ornaments of their houses, and of all their wares, goods, and chattel[s], the chief moveables, will be made common" (V. iii. 192–201).

Another parody of the speeches on the large and little worlds of man is aimed at Jonson's learned endeavors; however, Horace's metaphysical apostrophe to hair in Dekker's *Satiromastix* could stand as a gentle parody of Shakespeare as well:

> For, if of all the bodies parts, the head
> Be the most royall: If discourse, wit, Iudgement,
> And all our vnderstanding faculties,
> Sit there in their high Court of Parliament,
> Enacting lawes to sway this humorous world:
> This little Ile of Man: needes must that crowne,

Which stands vpon this supreame head, be faire.

(IV. i. 64–70)

And the speech goes on for thirty more lines! After *Hamlet*, philosophical apostrophes to man occur frequently. Chrisoganus observing war in Marston's *Histrio-mastix*, asks,

O, what a thing is man, that thus forgets
The end of his creation; and each houre
Strikes at the glory of his maker thus?   (pp. 291–292)

And Crites in Jonson's *Cynthia's Revels* laments,

O how despisde and base a thing is man,
If he not strive t'erect his groueling thoughts
Above the straine of flesh!   (I. v. 33–35)

Indeed these philosophical reflections were so abundant that a clown in the anonymous *Wisdome of Doctor Dodypoll* could seek a laugh by asking,

                    what is man?
A Pancake tost in Fortune's frying pan.   (p. 117)

Ulysses' finest speech, "One touch of nature makes the whole world kin," is concerned with man's fallen condition in a world of mutability, outer and inner, physical and mental. Gwalter in Dekker's *Patient Grissil* reflects the same concern:

Oh whats this world, but a confused throng
Of fooles and mad men, crowding in a thrust
To shoulder out the wise, trip downe the iust.

(III. i. 157–159)

And he seeks relentlessly to find a kind of stability and permanent value within the world. Feliche has a fourteen-line speech in Marston's *Antonio and Mellida* which reads almost line for line as a parody of Shakespeare's morally reassuring Sonnet 29, "When, in disgrace with Fortune," so diametrically opposed are the attitudes (p. 117). And Pandulfo's stoicism in *Antonios Reuenge* shows that he too has fallen beneath disillusion into such self-contented isolation that the affairs of man do not really concern him.

Crites in Jonson's *Cynthia's Revels* does not see much in life that pleases him; however, his philosophy is rooted in the same soil as is Ulysses';

> O vanitie,
> How are thy painted beauties doted on,
> By light, and emptie ideats! how pursu'de
> With open and extended appetite! . . .
> With the long irkesomenesse of following time!
>
> .   .   .   .
>
> But such is the peruersenesse of our nature,
> That if we once but fancie leuitie,
> (How antike and ridiculous so ere
> It sute with us) and yet will our muffled thought
> Choose rather not to see it, then auoide it.   (I. v. 24–59)

It is clear, then, that the philosophical speech is particularly common to these plays, and that latinate diction is a natural extension of its tendency to move on the abstract plane. In many ways the anonymous *Linqua* (1602), which could be called a dramatization of Sir John Davies' *Nosce Teipsum* (1599), typifies in the extreme this particular tendency. On the other hand, the plays of Chapman abound with reversals of traditional thought.[13] In fact one of Chapman's heroes even defends the usually scorned heavy use of cosmetics.[14] But his intellectual inversions emphasize just as much as does *Linqua* the degree to which philosophical interest is contained in these plays. Margaret in *The Gentleman Usher* is following tradition when she says that the "laws of God and Nature [are] more / Than formal

laws of men," but her disquisition proves only that the laws
of society do not bind her (IV. ii. 134–147). Strozza likewise proves that man should rule over and maintain order
in the microcosm, but that so doing disobliges him from
concern with order in the macrocosm (V. iv. 56–66).

In addition, the long, latinate flights from Chapman's
heroes afford evidence of the kind of style that was cap-
turing audiences in the private theaters. Clarence in *Sir Giles
Goosecap* meditates aloud:

> Work on, sweet love; I am not yet resolv'd
> T'exhaust this troubled spring of vanities
> And nurse of perturbations, my poor life;
> And therefore . . . I have chosen love
> To blind my reason with his misty hands
> And make my estimative power believe
> I have a project worthy to employ
> What worth so ever my whole man affords.   (I. iv. 1–13)

Even in anguish Marston's Pasquil in *Jacke Drums Entertainment* maintains an abstract manner of speaking:

> Go haste away, flie from the pestilence
> Of my contagious griefe . . .
> Oh thou omnipotent, infinitie,
> Crack not the sinewes of my patience
> With racking torment: Insist not thus to scourge
> My tender youth with sharpe affliction.   (p. 214)

Although words such as these could be the mark of a learned
man, many gallants in "these ignorant well-spoken days" [15]
seem to have aped learning through the use of elevated diction. Ralph's vocabulary in Munday's *Downfall of Robert,
Earl of Huntington* sounds so much like Hamlet's parody
of Osric that it comes as no surprise when he is ridiculed by

Skelton (pp. 135–137). Balurdo early in Marston's *Antonios Reuenge* picks up "retort and obtuse" and uses them throughout in every possible unlikely context (p. 77). Jonson, of course, goes one step further in *Poetaster* (V. iii), ridiculing Marston for straining after a learned vocabulary, even though he himself is quite latinate. The opening, serious dialogue in one scene in *Cynthia's Revels*, for example, contains *observance, satisfaction, profess, affectation, austerity,* and *prodigious* all couched in a latinate syntax (V. i. 1–11).

Because the anonymous *Wily Beguiled* is an obvious imitation of Jonson, it reveals what its author must have felt were the novel touches that his own play needed to be successful, and latinate diction was one. His scholar-lover talks about the "profound circumambulation of my supernatural wit," while his witty vice figure suggests to a country wench that "in a bouncing bravation,/ Let's talk of our copulation" and chastises a lout for having "made an infusion of your stinking excrements in your stalking implements" (pp. 321, 327, 241).

In this quotation of Will Cricket latinate diction is not used to make a generalized, but a blunt observation. The tone of the statement is not typical of Cricket, but it is of Thersites, the period's most bitter satiric commentator on the human scene. O. J. Campbell in *Comicall Satyre* and Alvin Kernan in *The Cankered Muse* have shown that the satiric observer was a popular figure in the private theater. Indeed, Shakespeare, Jonson, Chapman, and Marston all comment at the turn of the century on how the satiric vein was drawing patrons to all theaters. Kernan reminds us, however, that one can be satiric without writing a satire, and that the social ranks and specific attitudes of the railers were varied: Dekker's *Old Fortunatus* in many ways anticipates Jonson's *Cynthia's Revels* in the way in which it criticizes fanciful courtiers, but it is not a satire; and, as Campbell shows in

Comicall Satyre, Jonson even had different kinds of railers in a single play.

A sampling of public plays can illustrate the variety of forms and attitudes which these figures assumed. Captain Bonvile in Heywood's *Royall King, and the Loyall Subject* is a "rayling" satirist in almost every scene in which he appears; however, unlike Thersites he not only seems to have a justified reason for railing, but also has displayed moral worth in battle. Moreover, because he practices what he preaches, he does not alienate the audience: one prostitute is even converted from sin by him (p. 51). Patient Grissil's brother Laureo in Dekker's play is a miniature example of the melancholy scholars Maciliente, Chrisoganus, and Dowsecer who were Jonson's, Marston's, and Chapman's early satiric spokesmen:

> All *Italie* is full of them that snarle,
> And bay and barke at other mens abuse
> Let liue themselves like beastes in all abuse.
>
> . . . .
>
> Dost thou not see our wine-bellie drunkards reele?
> Our fat fed gluttons wallow in the streetes,
> Hauing no eyes but to behold their guts,
> No heads but braineless scalpes, no sence to smell,
> But where full feastes abound in all excesse
> These *Epimoei* be our *Epicures.*　　　　(V. i. 21–35)

Babulo's constant rejoinders, like the remarks of that "virtuous vice" Shadow in Dekker's *Old Fortunatus,* assert positive values; the clown in his *Sir Thomas Wyatt,* on the other hand, shows the moral insensitivity of Thersites. When Homes is struck with remorse after betraying his master, the rebel Suffolk, he comes back on stage *"with a Halter about his necke,"* movingly repents, buries the gold he has received, and hangs himself. The dignity of his death, however, is undercut by the clown who finds it highly amusing, takes the gold for himself, and goes off to London to buy new clothes, planning to "throwe this Dog in a Ditch" along the way (II. iii. 71–91).

What distinguishes Thersites from this clown are the strings of epithets and base similes that he applies to people. He is like Jonson's Carlo Buffone in *Every Man out of his Humour* who *"with absurd* simile's *will transforme any person into deformity"* (Preface), Chapman's Poggio in *The Gentleman Usher* whose "poison blisters [his] unhappy tongue" (I. i. 157), and Jonson's Tucca in *Poetaster* who curses people with diseases: "His moyles? now the *bots*, the *spauin*, and the *glanders*, and some dozen diseases more, light on him, and his moyles. What ha' they the *yellowes*, his moyles, that they come no faster? or are they foundred? ha? his moyles ha' the *staggers* belike: ha' they?" (I. ii. 174–178). Dekker's Tucca has a more colorful and varied vocabulary, but he can be just as low in coining invective against Horace: "His wittes are somewhat hard bound: The Puncke his Muse has sore labour ere the whoore bee deliuered: the poore saffron-cheeke Sunburnt Gipsie wantes Phisicke; giue the hungrie-face pudding-pye-eater ten Pilles: ten shillings my faire Angelica, they'l make his Muse as yare as a tumbler" (*Satiromastix*, I. ii. 366–370).

CONCLUSION

Because Ulysses traditionally was called sly and politic and because he accomplishes little but speaks at length in *Troilus and Cressida* many modern critics have concluded that Ulysses is supposed to be ridiculous and boring. Neither of these effects is intentional. When he talks about the world picture and the human condition, Ulysses says nothing that is not sound and serious Elizabethan philosophy; if he is boring to us in his exposition of these felt beliefs of Christian humanism, we should remember that, in general, Elizabethan audiences must have been attentive or playwrights would not have written so many lengthy dramatic speeches. Madeleine Doran has shown in *Endeavors of Art* how the rhetorical debate of the grammar school evolved as a convention of drama and Gladys D. Willcock further suggests that some of the audience's "capacity for attention may be credited to rhetoric in its religious context. Children trained to recapitulate on Monday Sunday's hour-long discourse might find Hamlet, Ulysses, or Coriolanus admirably pointed and brief." [16] Mention of *Hamlet* should remind us, moreover, that the number and length of philosophical speeches in the canon increase as one approaches *Troilus and Cressida*, and that this Shakespearean phenomenon is in keeping with the emphasis on strong, learned speeches in the plays around *Troilus*.

W. W. Lawrence correctly observed that Shakespeare was aware that "an ability to decorate intellectual flights with elaborate phraseology was a fashionable accomplishment of the day"; [17] however, the kind of learning which Shakespeare embellished was generally the positive humanism of his age. Even Hamlet did not condemn the world just because he was unhappy in it. On the other hand, the long speeches in the private theaters tend to reflect the fashionable turn-of-the-century Neo-Stoicism. In light of the fact that Agamemnon opens the Greek council with a labored speech recommending a stoic acceptance of the Grecian failure to take Troy, one is tempted to find in Ulysses' speech on order Shakespeare's fervent defense of the unwritten constitution of his age which was being undermined in several areas, including the playhouses across the river. We have noted that there is a possible reference to the current theatrical scene in Ulysses' description of Achilles and Patroclus in retirement. Viewed against the kind of hero being presented

in the coterie plays, an otherwise puzzling statement of
Ajax can be explained if we believe that Shakespeare was
fully aware of the rival traditions reflected in the War of
the Theatres. Having accused Achilles of pride, Ajax notes,
"You may call it melancholy, if you will favour the man"
(II. iii. 94–95).

But it is not necessary to search for examples of disorder
exterior to the play for Ulysses to analyze; the Troy legend
was full of them. In addition to providing the subject matter
for Ulysses and Hector to develop, the Troy material was
filled with councils and debates in which speeches like theirs
in the play are reported at length. If he needed it, Shakespeare also had the general examples of Lydgate and Chapman, each of whom shaped the story of Troy in such a
way that it illustrated moral and ethical principles. But over
all, in every source, the legend of Troy was an *exemplum*
of disaster through disorder, moral and ethical; as a result,
regardless of how persuasive and erudite Ulysses might be,
the facts of history could not be changed.

These mutually reinforcing influences, then, lie behind
the play: positive, Shakespearean philosophy, a theatrical
demand for strong speeches, and a story that emphasized
debate — all of which work against the negative nature of
the material and its traditional significance. Understanding
that this contradiction exists in the background of the play
can help us to understand more clearly the predicament of
Hector during and at the end of the council scene.

Alfred Harbage has pointed out that "Shakespeare has no
hesitation, in cases where personal dignity or courage is concerned — the honor of soldiers — to let estimable men see
the morally superior side and choose the inferior one. What
he does in such cases is to withhold condemnation from the
men, but picture fully the merits of the rejected course. Then
we can think as we please." [18] This is certainly Shakespeare's

plan with regard to Hector; however, the twofold demand of following the debate convention and of adhering to the story pulls the alternatives offered so widely apart that Hector's switch from contemplative statesman to active warrior creates an aesthetic shock. As Madeleine Doran succinctly observes: "Shakespeare lets interest in the debate momentarily run away with the necessities of his plot." [19]

The problem afforded by the demand for long and learned speeches and the negative nature of the story could have been solved easily by Shakespeare had he been willing to cast those speeches in a negative mode. To have done so would have meant the sacrificing the virtue of personal belief to the convenience of commercial expedience and, even though he weakened his play, Shakespeare did not make the attempt. Indeed, even Agamemnon's speech is in the vein of Vergilian stoicism rather than a copy of Marston's rant.

It has been suggested by Harbage that Shakespeare's audience might have made an association between the voice of Marston and the voice of Thersites.[20] There is no doubt that Thersites fulfills his traditional role of railing detractor, just as there is little doubt that Marston was himself a true railing detractor.[21] Marston was certainly a melancholic malcontent, but we can never know if he was as misanthropic as Thersites is.[22] Alvin Kernan in *The Cankered Muse* has shown, and we have seen, that Marston's and Jonson's plays of this period had many envious detractors, as did the plays of Shakespeare especially after *As You Like It*; but even Parolles in *All's Well* does not sink so low as Thersites.

O. J. Campbell believes that Thersites' role is to keep the audience in a spirit of derision, but that "if he is offensive in the discharge of his dramatic duties, that is because Shakespeare's higher emotional intensity and superiority in imagination lend to characters, endurable in the art of lesser men, qualities that are aesthetically unacceptable." [23] More specifically, Kernan shows how Thersites has all the characteristics of the turn-of-the-century satyr satirist: "Thersites is a malevolent force, a type of primal hatred and pride, and what Shakespeare has done is to take the conventional character of the satirist and strip away his pretensions to being a moral healer and intensify his basic loathing of all mankind." [24] The typing is all the more strong because, as we saw, the name of Thersites was synonymous with a rhetorical mode of violent railing. When Shakespeare broke the conventional molds of the braggart soldier and the miserly Jew, he breathed life into sympathetic human beings, but here he created a most despicable kind of person, one who takes fragments and suggestions of truths and distorts them into the appearance of whole truth. But it is the ugly diatribes of Thersites, along with the elevated, latinate speeches of Ulysses, which provide the strongest indication that Shakespeare in 1601 was fully and alertly aware of prevailing theatrical fashions both in the private and in the public theaters.

CHAPTER VIII · CONCLUSION AND EPILOGUE

*F*INAL EVIDENCE that in writing *Troilus and Cressida* Shakespeare had his eye on the rival repertories of both the public and the private theaters lies in the fact that his play is the only extant work about the Trojan War in English which tries to tell with equal emphasis the stories of the lovers and the siege. Chaucer and Henryson focused on Troilus and Cressida and kept war in the background, but Lydgate, Caxton, Peele in *The Tale of Troy* (1589), the author of the Admiral's fragment, and Heywood in his *Iron Age* (1609) all but exclude the love story. Except for brief mention of the affair as pitiable but morally lamentable they kept their attention on the war story; Troilus and Cressida's was simply not the kind of tale which mixed with heroic romance. Although their story, as Coleridge remarked, can hardly be imagined in any kind of dramatic presentation other than Shakespeare's, the atmosphere of decadence which surrounds the love scenes of Ilium and Pandarus' house is not conducive to the heroic, romantic mode which in the public mind was associated with the Trojan war. The inference is inescapable that Shakespeare did not have to tell both branches of the Troy legend which literary tradition offered him merely because he wished to write a play on Troy, and especially if he wished fully to imitate his coterie rivals.

The two branches do not complement each other, and Shakespeare seems to have been uncomfortable in his attempts to bring them together. By choosing the love of Troilus for Cressida as managed by Pandarus in the decadent atmosphere of a court which honored the love of Paris for

Helen, and as undone by Diomedes in the disordered Grecian camp, Shakespeare was able to match all the illicit and passionate affairs which the private theaters put on the boards; in so doing, however, he neither sacrificed his own principles nor disturbed those of his audience, for his characters' destinies were firmly fixed in the minds of his spectators. In fact, the love story was so morally "safe" in this respect that Marston had ridiculed the public stage in *Histrio-mastix*, his first play for Paul's in 1599, by presenting the burlesque love scene between a Troilus and a Cressida. Still Shakespeare emphasized early in his play the proverbial falsity of Cressida, the blind loyalty of Troilus, and the base role of panders so that the end of the love plot and the proper judgment of its participants were never in doubt. Thus if Shakespeare was imitating the theater of the coterie, again, it was not slavishly and blindly.

This ambivalence or half-imitation shows up again and again. He wanted a satiric spokesman, but took one who could not possibly be associated with his own voice. He introduced stylized, latinate rhetoric, but cast it in a traditional, positive vein. He created a prurient old man to conduct the illicit love affair, but when after Pandarus says in the Paris-Helen scene, "I come to speak with Paris from the Prince Troilus. I will make a complimental assault upon him, for my business seethes" (III. i. 40–43), the page's parting aside is so in keeping with Shakespeare's unconscious morality and healthy sense of humor that we catch a possible criticism of the author's creations made by the author himself: "Sodden business! There's a stew'd phrase indeed!"

One could go on and on pointing out how elements in the play reflect the rival public and private traditions outside the play; but parallels do not prove intentions. What is needed is external evidence more specific than that yet used in order to be sure what Shakespeare had in mind in writing *Troilus and Cressida*. The closest thing to this kind of separate, authoritative statement is Shakespeare's prologue. In general it prepares us for the play. The diction is sometimes noble and romantic, sometimes mocking. In medieval manner the gates of Troy all are named, in a serious manner the siege is called a "cruel war," but in a lighter vein we are told that,

> The ravish'd Helen, Menelaus' queen,
> With wanton Paris sleeps, and that's the quarrel.

Finally, the general attitude which we are to assume and which governs the development of the play is summarized in conclusion:

> Now expectation, tickling skittish spirits
> On one and other side, Troyan and Greek,
> Sets all on hazard.

But there follows the more personal address to the "fair beholders." The speaker mocks the auctorial audacity recently displayed by Ben Jonson in the prologue to his *Poetaster* by saying that he also may be

> A Prologue armed, but not in confidence
> Of author's pen or actor's voice, but suited
> In like conditions as our argument.

The technique of multiple reference in this last line to the War of the Theatres and to the play itself is amplified in the closing couplet to the prologue. Here Shakespeare indicates several things. First he continues to offer a genial ethos before the audience in contrast to Jonson's rudeness, and implies that it is a matter of luck and neither author's nor audience's fault if a play, good or bad, does not please. Secondly he implies that the members of the audience must make their own moral judgments concerning the action of the play. And lastly, he betrays some uneasiness in offering a play based on traditionally popular material but which uses some of the aesthetic novelties being developed and emphasized by the poets' war which took place within the larger commercial war for audiences:

> Like, or find fault; do as your pleasures are:
> Now good or bad, 'tis but the chance of war.

For better or worse, in writing *Troilus and Cressida* Shakespeare attempted to meet the current demands of "box-office" by presenting "new trickes" along with "that old *Decorum*."

EPILOGUE

D. A. Traversi has suggested that Shakespeare intended in *Troilus and Cressida* to subject traditional romance materials to ridicule, but that he was neither confident nor comfortable in the mock heroic and that his uncertainty of purpose is apparent even in the Prologue. If Shakespeare was uncertain, his audience must have been, and his critics have been. The wide diversity of interpretation of *Troilus* can be traced to the abundance of points of view from which critics may work, and the root reason for this abundance is almost accidental, a curious outgrowth of the theatrical scene of 1598 to 1603. It may seem paradoxical, but if Shakespeare were not a consummate artist, *Troilus and Cressida* would afford no critical difficulties. Shakespeare never merely followed the lead of others or merely copied conventions; if he had, *Troilus and Cressida* would not be the dramatic failure that it is, but would have been successfully shaped either as a private or a public play.

As it stands, then, *Troilus and Cressida* is a critical problem, but the very fact that we pay so much attention to it is proof enough that it is not an artistic failure. Unfortunately, too many critics have been content to say with Hazlitt in

Characters of Shakespear's Plays (1817) that *Troilus* is "one of the most loose and desultory of our author's plays: it rambles on just as it happens, but it overtakes, together with some indifferent matter, a prodigious number of fine things in its way," and then go on to elucidate the "fine things" while ignoring the challenge to put the play as a whole into a meaningful category.

In spite of the Elizabethan tendency to accept the matter of Troy as history, *Troilus* is not a history play and not merely because we do not think of ourselves as Trojans. Nothing really *happens* in the play; things merely take place. There is nothing of the inevitable in the action, only the accidental. There is no feeling of a forward thrust of events; one thing just follows another. To a degree, much of this could be said of *Hamlet*, but there the negative effect of the mundane is counteracted by the complexity and magnitude of Hamlet's personality. *Hamlet* works as a tragedy simply because we can easily share in Hamlet's problems. But *Troilus and Cressida* is not a tragedy because we not only are not swept up in the action, but we cannot identify ourselves with any of the characters: the love plot is so staged that we must come to the mismatched lovers through Pandarus, Thersites' sketches of the Greeks hold in check any inherent feeling we might have for their Homeric nobility, and Hector's contradictory behavior in the face of the demands of war and public honor on one hand and of domestic love and private honor on the other complicates but does not enrich his characterization. A. C. Bradley summed up this sense of alienation from action, dialogue, and character by saying that "a spirit of bitterness and contempt seems to pervade" the play; although it incorporates "an intense intellectual activity, . . . a certain coldness and hardness" preclude the possibility of a tragic effect.[1] We are forced, in short, to view the play with detachment.

Because detachment is the *sine qua non* of comedy, the question naturally arises, is *Troilus* that? Certainly it is not the romantic comedy of the early period nor is it the comedy of romance of the late plays because its rituals are self-contained. Is it, then, comical satire as O. J. Campbell long ago suggested? An affirmative answer is possible here only if it is heavily qualified, for one simply cannot ignore the great amount of heroic pageantry and serious debate, public, semipublic, and private, which abound. When Hector and Achilles first meet face to face we watch in awe the confrontation of two cultures, of two worlds; and even such a stock figure of ridicule as Cressida raises questions concerning herself and her conduct which interrupt from time to time the flow of automatic satiric response to force the audience to be reflective. Thus we are come full circle and must, along with Boas and Shaw, W. W. Lawrence and E. M. W. Tillyard, call *Troilus and Cressida* a problem play as that term has been defined in drama and criticism since Strindberg and Ibsen.

Such a label would have had little meaning in Shakespeare's day — after all, all plays were problem plays — and the fact remains that *Troilus and Cressida* was an anomaly in and of its age. Still, in sitting down under the pressure of serious theatrical competition to work with almost intractable material Shakespeare responded automatically to the challenge. He breathed life into traditional figures; his themes of love and lust, war and honor, order and disorder are all mutually reinforcing; and the plots in which they originate all come together. In addition, the idea that true worthiness is an ethical attribute as well as a moral concern is emphasized in order to unite all the themes and characters. But another theme, that of Time the common arbitrator, the force in life which works to defeat our successive expectations, as well as the inconclusive plot and the recurring work-a-day diction of digestion and disease, all tend to prevent our being drawn emotionally into the action of the play. Because of its complexity and the manner in which it is presented, we are forced to view the play objectively. *Troilus and Cressida* was a failure, but a failure mainly because the age was not ready for a drama which employed the comic stance of moral objectivity in a discursive manner *vis-à-vis* the facts of life. Such a mode demands a high degree of social awareness, a broad secularization of the kind that produced and encouraged the novel. If *Troilus and Cressida* was caviare, it was so not just to the general.

Critics and scholars such as Coleridge and Dowden, Charles Williams and Allardyce Nicoll have instinctively felt that *Troilus and Cressida* contains a great deal of formal experimentation, and because Shakespeare was forced out of his usual modes in writing *Troilus* we can now see that such conjectures are just. Moreover, in his study of Shakespeare's growing use of learning, Virgil Whitaker concludes that the play is "the keystone in the arch of Shakespeare's intellectual development, however rough-hewn and misshapen it may be." [2] Seen in the light of this larger, aesthetic context *Troilus and Cressida* again is clearly not a failure. Coming as it does midway in Shakespeare's career, it proved to be a kind of watershed for the collecting of the force and power needed for the creation of the final magnificent tragedies and late romances. Indeed, the fact that *Troilus* comes halfway through Shakespeare's career but two-thirds of the way through the canon should remind us to what a great extent the last plays are so completely Shakespearean while the earlier ones are so very Elizabethan. In *Troilus and Cressida* Shakespeare found and improved upon many of the techniques which matured his art.

The most important aspect of *Troilus* in relation to the later plays was the way in which Shakespeare began to fuse public idea and inner emotion within the action of a tragedy.

Eliot was correct in asserting that character tends to remain separate from and to dominate action in *Hamlet*, though wrong in denying the epithet great to a work so obviously engaging in its portrayal of the hero that Aristotle's very practical observation on action for once can be ignored. But in Troilus, a lesser Hamlet figure, idea and emotion merge in the end with the action, such as that action is, when Troilus discovers that his simple, abstract philosophy cannot deal with complicated reality. Furthermore we have seen how the over-all plot of the play is woven with thematic material which complements the three threads of action, and even the action, so seemingly disparate, has its parallel touches: Troilus plays private and public roles, Achilles, because of private, emotional reasons, allows the national interest of the Greeks to go unattended and Hector ignores his domestic obligations in order to further the national interest of the Trojans — albeit for reasons even more selfish than Achilles'. This kind of public-private debate within a man's soul, the necessity of choosing between mutually exclusive — at least apparently so — alternatives, lies at the heart of Shakespearean tragedy. Although the experimental structure of *Troilus* precluded tight union of thought, character, and action, when Shakespeare returned to the basic morality pattern for the plots of *Othello, Macbeth,* and *Lear* he was able to introduce early the thought of the action and to develop character within the action in such a way that the completely fused emotional, intellectual anguish of recognition on the hero's part of his sin — ignorance, human weakness, or call it what you will — is in turn felt and shared by the audience. And because the depth of the despair experienced by Lear is marked by the intensity of his diction when in disgust and madness he cries out against the human comedy that is life, perhaps we can excuse the existence of a Thersites.

When in *Timon of Athens* Shakespeare planned a play

with a near-Thersites figure as the hero he seems to have
dropped the plan, but the alienation we feel from Coriolanus stems in part from his similarity to Thersites. Interestingly O. J. Campbell in *Shakespeare's Satire* has related the
general satiric vein of *Troilus and Cressida* to *Coriolanus*
and because he sees the latter as basically a serious play
his reading of it is much more impressive than is his reading of *Troilus*. Surely central to both is the question of one's
loyalties to two worlds, one's own world of man and the
community of men.

No play in the canon makes a more rigorous examination
of this question than does *Antony and Cleopatra*, and no
play in the canon is more closely related to *Troilus and
Cressida*. The concerns of love and lust, war and honor, order
and disorder all appear separately; the values of the Roman
World and Egyptian are opposed; and the action of the
play is diffuse and has several false climaxes and sudden
turns. Enobarbus in his railing even resembles Thersites a
little — but only a little, for he has also the intelligence and
human concern of Ulysses. But most important, the roles of
Troilus, Hector, and Achilles meet in Antony while Helen
and Cressida are Cleopatra; hence the play holds its focus
steadily on the problem of allegiance and achieves a depth
of emotion which *Troilus* does not. Still, the complexity
of response which *Antony and Cleopatra* evokes must in
part be traced to the fact that in *Troilus and Cressida* Shakespeare forced himself to work beyond his usual modes and
attitudes.

Because of this extension, when Shakespeare moved into
the unreal worlds of the late romances he could keep them
believable by populating them with realists: Iachimo, as
well as Iago, has gone to school to Thersites. Even the lust-
blinded Leontes in the first half of *The Winter's Tale* is a
kind of satiric railer against women. But what separates

Cymbeline, *The Winter's Tale*, and *The Tempest* from *Troilus and Cressida* is their setting in a mythic world. Here, as Madeleine Doran has observed, by retreating from the real world Shakespeare was able finally to discuss real social and ethical problems and at the same time come to aesthetically satisfying resolutions of plot. Indeed, one of the main lessons Shakespeare seems to have learned from *Troilus and Cressida* and the other "problem plays" is the one he seems to have learned from the Lancastrian cycle: because the stage is not a "real" place, it should not be set too literally as such. The dramatist must build his artifice out of fiction, and then his audience will grant him this *donnée* only in proportion to his lack of insistence on it. Hence by drawing upon the audience's initial suspension of disbelief the dramatist can take the audience in any direction he wants to go. By returning to the morality pattern of native English tragedy and the imaginary world of native English comedy Shakespeare capitalized upon the basic symbolic value of his stage. The two modes allowed him to talk either about everyman somewhere or all men everywhere. In this regard Shakespeare was moving against the current of his time because, as Bernard Spivak has so admirably suggested in *Shakespeare and the Allegory of Evil*, "the conventions of his stage are on a pilgrimage . . . toward naturalism," toward the "dramatic imitation of literal life and historical event."[3] If we are to understand fully the phenomena of *Troilus and Cressida*, or the other problem plays, here is the best lead to follow: it suggests a context beyond the play itself and beyond the development of the author.

It is in this final context that Shakespeare's play is an ultimate success. As Shaw remarked, in *Troilus and Cressida* Shakespeare seemed ready to start the twentieth century, and it is no accident that *Troilus* has gained fame only in our time, for we are used to the mode of presentation — "the comedy of pure mind" Arthur Symons called it in what is probably the most sensitive critical response to the play — and the subject matter seems all too contemporary because, again as Symons observed, "it is made out of history, with an infinite deal of tragedy in the matter of it, and its upshot is purely comic." [4] Or, as Heine observed, the muse of Tragedy is "perceptible everywhere in this play, except that here, for once, she would be gay and act the clown." [5] *Troilus and Cressida* is comedy, but neither festive nor typal, only human. It tries neither to excuse nor to explain human behavior; it simply observes and reports. It almost could be presented in today's Theater of the Absurd.[6]

Such a conclusion is not intended to startle; rather it should only remind us that we are in the presence of genius. Una Ellis-Fermor's confession in *The Frontiers of Drama* regarding *Troilus and Cressida* is particularly revealing in this context. She said that she was "for many years satisfied to see in this play a momentary failure of Shakespeare's powers," but that after many more years of studying the play she came to the realization that *"Troilus and Cressida* is not a great failure to record a phase of experience *beyond the scope of dramatic form*, but a great achievement, perhaps one of the greatest, in the expression of that phase, *transcending those limitations to produce a living work of art."* [7] In other words, as my italics emphasize, the more *Troilus and Cressida* is studied not as drama but as a philosophic work of art, latent aspects of its particular ethos become clear. Miss Ellis-Fermor's ensuing analysis of and commentary on the various dialectics are brilliant both with regard to the implications of Shakespeare's text and its relevance in the modern world, and her approach is certainly a valid one. But she need not have rejected her initial, instinctive response to *Troilus* as drama in order to make her explication because a play may be a failure and a work of art. If this simple observation could be accepted, future literature on *Troilus and Cressida* would bring to an end both question-begging of its origins and success, and narrow, only specially revealing approaches to its content.

If we are ever to understand this complex play in *all* contexts we must be flexible and receptive in our response to it. Clifford Leech, discussing the "capability" of Shakespeare, says concerning plays such as *Troilus*: "Tragedy and comedy, as modes of perception determining the general pattern of the thing perceived, regulate the poet's responses to the world and receive his (not total but) firm allegiance. When, however, we enter a territory less clearly charted than tragic or comic drama, we should strictly avoid the imposition of convenient patterns. We should be neutral in the play's debates, at least to the extent that Shakespeare was; above all, we should not tamper with the text so as to make plain a 'message' that Shakespeare did not fully assert." [8] Alfred Harbage, as Leech remarks, has made the same appeal with regard to all of Shakespeare, but the plea has special pertinence with regard to this play. Unlike most of Shakespeare, *Troilus and Cressida* proved to be a play not for its age, but for all of time.

BIBLIOGRAPHY OF PRIMARY SOURCES

An Alarum for London, ed. W. W. Greg. Malone Society Reprints, London, 1913.

Armin, Robert. *The Fool and The Ice*, ed. J. O. Halliwell-Phillips. London, 1883.

Benoît de Sainte-More. *Le roman de Troie*, ed. Léopold Constans. 6 vols. Paris, Firmin Didot and Co., 1904–1912.

Boccaccio, Giovanni. *The Filostrato*, a translation with parallel texts by N. E. Griffin and A. B. Myrick. Philadelphia, University of Pennsylvania Press, and London, Oxford University Press, 1929.

Bradshaw, Thomas. *The Sheperd's Starre*. London, 1591.

Bullen, A. H., ed. *A Collection of Old Plays*. 4 vols. London, 1882–1885.

Captain Thomas Stukeley, ed. Simpson (q.v.). Vol. I.

Caxton, William. *The Recuyell of the Historyes of Troye, written in French by Raoul Lefèvre, tr. and printed by William Caxton*, ed. Heinrich Oskar Sommer. 2 vols. London, 1894.

Chapman, George. *The Gentleman Usher*, ed. Thomas M. Parrott. *The Comedies of George Chapman*. London, E. P. Dutton, 1914.

———— *Sir Giles Goosecap*, ed. T. M. Parrott.

———— *An Humorous Day's Mirth*, ed. T. M. Parrott.

———— *Homer*, ed. Allardyce Nicoll. 2 vols. New York, Pantheon Books, 1956.

Chaucer, Geoffrey. *The Poetical Works*, ed. F. N. Robinson. Cambridge, Massachusetts, Houghton Mifflin, 1933.

Chettle, Henry. *Hoffman*, ed. Harold Jenkins. Malone Society Reprints, London, 1950.

Cox, Leonard. *The Arte or Crafte of Rhethoryke*, ed. Frederic I. Carpenter. Chicago, 1899.

Dares Phrygius. *De Excidio Troiae historia*, ed. F. Meister. Leipzig, 1873.

Davies, Sir John. *Poems*, reproduced in facsimile by Clare Howard. New York, Columbia University Press, 1941.

Day, John, Henry Chettle, and William Haughton. *The Blind Beggar of Bednal Green*, ed. J. S. Farmer. Tudor Facsimile Texts, London, 1914.

Dekker, Thomas. *Old Fortunatus*, ed. F. T. Bowers. *The Dramatic Works of Thomas Dekker*. 4 vols. Cambridge, England, Cambridge University Press, 1953–1961. Vol. I.

—— *Patient Grissil*, ed. F. T. Bowers. Vol. I.

—— *Satiromastix*, ed. F. T. Bowers. Vol. I.

—— *The Shoemakers Holiday*, ed. F. T. Bowers. Vol. I.

—— *Sir Thomas Wyatt*, ed. F. T. Bowers. Vol. I.

Dictys Cretensis. *Ephemeridos belli Troiani*, ed. F. Meister. Leipzig, 1872.

Dodsley, Robert. *A Select Collection of Old English Plays*, ed. W. Carew Hazlitt. 15 vols. London, 1874–1876.

Donne, John. *The Poems*, ed. H. J. C. Grierson. 2 vols. Oxford, Clarendon Press, 1912.

Drayton, Michael, Richard Hathaway, Anthony Munday, and Robert Wilson. *1 Sir John Oldcastle*, ed. W. Carew Hazlitt. *The Doubtful Plays of William Shakespeare*. London, n.d.

Dryden, John. *Troilus and Cressida: or, Truth Found too Late*, ed. Sir Walter Scott, rev. ed. George Saintsbury. *The Dramatic Works of John Dryden*. 18 vols. Edinburgh, 1882–1892. Vol. VI.

Gibson, Anthony. *A Womans Worth*. London, 1599.

Greene, Robert. *Euphues, His Censure to Philautus*, ed. A. B. Grosart. *The Life and Complete Works in Prose and Verse*. 15 vols. London, 1881–1886. Vol. VI.

Guido de Columnis. *Historia destructionis Troiae*, ed. N. E. Griffin. Cambridge, Massachusetts, The Mediaeval Academy of America, 1936.

Hall, Joseph. *Poems*, ed. A. Davenport. Liverpool, University Press, 1949.

Henryson, Robert. *The Testament of Cresseid*, ed. Bruce Dickins. London, Faber and Faber, 1925, 1943.

Henslowe, Philip. *Diary*, ed. W. W. Greg. 2 vols. London, 1904–1908.

—— *Papers*, ed. W. W. Greg. London, 1907.

Heywood, Thomas. *An Apology for Actors*. Shakespeare Society Reprint, London, 1841.

—— *1* and *2 Edward IV*. *The Dramatic Works*. 6 vols. London, 1874. Vol. I.

—— *The Faire Maid of the Exchange*. Vol. II.

—— *The Foure Prentises of London*. Vol. II.

—— *The Iron Age*. Vol. III.

—— *Pleasant Dialogues and Drammas*. Vol. VI.

—— *Royall King, and the Loyall Subject*. Vol. VI.

——— *A Woman Killed With Kindnesse.* Vol. II.

——— *Troia Britanica: or, Great Britaines Troy.* London, 1609.

Hooker, Richard. *Of the Laws of Ecclesiastical Polity.* 2 vols. Everyman's Library, London, 1907, 1954.

How a Man May Choose a Good Wife from a Bad, ed. Dodsley (q.v.). Vol. IX.

I. O. *The Lamentation of Troy for the Death of Hector,* ed. E. C. Wilson. Institute of Elizabethan Studies, Chicago, 1959.

Jonson, Ben. *The Case is Alterd,* ed. C. H. Herford and Percy Simpson. *Ben Jonson.* 11 vols. Oxford, 1925–1952. Vol. III.

——— *Cynthia's Revels,* ed. Herford and Simpson. Vol. IV.

——— *Every Man in his Humour,* ed. Herford and Simpson. Vol. III.

——— *Every Man out of his Humour,* ed. Herford and Simpson. Vol. III.

——— *Poetaster,* ed. Herford and Simpson. Vol. IV.

Lefèvre, Raoul. *Recueil des Histoires de Troyes.* See Caxton.

Lingua, ed. Dodsley (q.v.). Vol. IX.

Look About You, ed. Dodsley (q.v.). Vol. VII.

Lydgate, John. *Troy Book,* ed. Henry Bergen. 4 vols. Early English Text Society, Extra Series, London, 1906–1935.

Marlowe, Christopher. "Hero and Leander," ed. Hyder E. Rollins and Herschel C. Baker. *The Renaissance in England.* Boston, D. C. Heath and Co., 1954, pp. 388–396.

Marston, John. *Antonio and Mellida,* ed. H. Harvey Wood. *The Plays of John Marston.* 3 vols. London, Oliver and Boyd, 1934–1939. Vol. I.

——— *Antonios Reuenge,* ed. H. H. Wood. Vol. I.

——— *Histrio-mastix,* ed. H. H. Wood. Vol. III.

——— *Jacke Drums Entertainment,* ed. H. H. Wood. Vol. III.

——— *What You Will,* ed. H. H. Wood. Vol. II.

——— *Poems,* ed. A. H. Bullen. *The Works of John Marston.* 3 vols. London, 1887. Vol. III.

The Maydes Metamorphosis, ed. Bullen (q.v.). Vol. I.

The Merry Devil of Edmonton, ed. Dodsley (q.v.). Vol. X.

Middleton, Thomas. *Blurt, Master-Constable,* ed. Bullen. *The Works of Thomas Middleton.* 8 vols. London, 1885. Vol. I.

——— *The Family of Love,* ed. Bullen. Vol. III.

Munday, Anthony. *The Downfall of Robert, Earl of Huntington,* ed. Dodsley (q.v.). Vol. VIII.

—— and Henry Chettle. *The Death of Robert, Earl of Huntington*, ed. Dodsley (q.v.). Vol. VIII.

Peele, George. *The Tale of Troy*, ed. David H. Horne. *The Life and Minor Works of George Peele*. New Haven, Yale University Press, 1952.

Porter, Henry. *The Two Angry Women of Abingdon*, ed. Dodsley (q.v.). Vol. VII.

The Rare Triumphs of Love and Fortune, ed. Dodsley (q.v.). Vol. VI.

2 The Return from Parnassus, ed. J. B. Leishman. *The Three Parnassus Plays*, London, Nicholson & Watson, 1949.

Rowlands, Samuel. *The Letting of Hvmors Blood in the Head-Vaine*, reprinted by James Ballantyne. Edinburgh, 1815.

Shakespeare, William. *Comedies, Histories, & Tragedies*, a facsimile edition of the First Folio prepared by Helge Kökeritz, with an introduction by Charles Tyler Prouty. New Haven, Yale University Press, 1954.

—— *The Complete Works*, ed. George L. Kittredge. Boston, Ginn & Co., 1936.

—— *A New Variorum Edition of Shakespeare: Troilus and Cressida*, ed. Harold N. Hillebrand and Thomas W. Baldwin. Philadelphia, J. B. Lippincott & Co., 1953.

—— *Troilus and Cressida: First Quarto, 1609*, a collotype facsimile prepared by W. W. Greg. The Shakespeare Association, London, 1952.

Shirley, James. *The Contention of Ajax and Ulysses for the Armour of Achilles*, ed. A. C. Dyce. *The Dramatic Works and Poems of James Shirley*. 6 vols. London, 1833. Vol. VI.

Sidney, Sir Philip. *The Defence of Poesy*, ed. Hyder E. Rollins and Herschel C. Baker. *The Renaissance in England*. Boston, D. C. Heath and Co., 1954. pp. 605–624.

Simpson, Richard, ed. *The School of Shakespeare*. 2 vols. New York, 1878.

Thersites, A New Interlude, called, ed. Dodsley (q.v.). Vol. I.

The Tryall of Chevalry, ed. Bullen (q.v.). Vol. III.

A Warning for Faire Women, ed. Simpson (q.v.). Vol. II.

The Weakest Goeth to the Wall, ed. W. W. Greg. Malone Society Reprints, London, 1912.

Whetstone, George. *The Rocke of Regard*, ed. J. P. Collier. London, 1867.

Wily Beguiled, ed. Dodsley (q.v.). Vol. IX.

The Wisdome of Doctor Dodypoll, ed. Bullen (q.v.). Vol. III.

NOTES

Chapter I. Introduction

1. W. W. Lawrence, *Shakespeare's Problem Comedies* (New York: Macmillan, 1931); E. M. W. Tillyard, *Shakespeare's Problem Plays* (London: Chatto & Windus, 1950); A. P. Rossiter, "The Problem Plays," *Angel with Horns*, ed. Graham Storey (London: Longmans, 1961), pp. 108–128; Ernest Schanzer, *The Problem Plays of Shakespeare* (London: Routledge & Kegan Paul, 1963).

2. J. H. Penniman, ed., *"Poetaster," by Ben Jonson, and "Satiromastix," by Thomas Dekker* (Boston: D. C. Heath, 1913); R. A. Small, *The Stage-Quarrel between Ben Jonson and the So-Called Poetasters* (Breslau: *Forschungen zur englischen sprache und literatur,* vol. I, 1899); Robert B. Sharpe, *The Real War of the Theatres: Shakespeare's Fellows in Rivalry with the Admiral's Men, 1594–1603: Repertories, Devices, and Types* (Boston: D. C. Heath, 1935); Alfred Harbage, *Shakespeare and the Rival Traditions* (New York: Macmillan, 1952); Robert Ornstein, *The Moral Vision of Jacobean Tragedy* (Madison: University of Wisconsin Press, 1960); John J. Enck, "The Peace of the Poetomachia," *PMLA*, 77:386–396 (September 1962); William W. Main, "Dramaturgical Norms in the Elizabethan Repertory," *SP*, 54:128–148 (April 1957), and "Character Amalgams in Shakespeare's *Troilus and Cressida*," *SP*, 58:170–178 (April 1961); and Margaret Swanson Lacy, "The Jacobean Problem Play: A Study of Shakespeare's *Measure for Measure* and *Troilus and Cressida* in Relation to Selected Plays of Chapman, Dekker, and Marston," unpub. diss., University of Wisconsin, 1956.

3. J. S. P. Tatlock, "The Chief Problem in Shakespeare," *The Sewanee Review*, 24:129–147 (April 1916), and "The Siege of Troy in Elizabethan Literature, Especially in Shakespeare and Heywood," *PMLA*, 30:673–770 (December 1915); Hyder E. Rollins, "The Troilus-Cressida Story from Chaucer to Shakespeare," *PMLA*, 32:383–429 (September 1917); Robert K. Presson, *Shakespeare's* TROILUS AND CRESSIDA *&* *The Legends of Troy* (Madison: University of Wisconsin Press, 1953); Edwin Eliott Willoughby, *The Printing of the First Folio of Shakespeare* (Oxford: Bibliographical Society, 1932); Samuel A. Tannenbaum, "A Critique of the Text of 'Troilus and Cressida': Part I, The Quarto Text," *The Shakespeare Association Bulle-*

tin, 9:55–74 (April 1934), and "Part II, The Folio Text," *Sh. Assoc. Bull.*, 9:125–144 and 198–214 (July and October 1934); Philip Williams, "The 'Second Issue' of Shakespeare's *Troilus and Cressida*, 1609," *Studies in Bibliography*, II (1949), 25–33, and "Shakespeare's *Troilus and Cressida*: The Relationship of Quarto and Folio," *Studies in Bibliography*, III (1950), 131–143; Alice Walker, "The Textual Problem of 'Troilus and Cressida'," *MLR*, 45:459–464 (October 1950); Oscar James Campbell, *Comicall Satyre and Shakespeare's* TROILUS AND CRESSIDA (San Marino, Calif.: Huntington Library Publications, 1938); H. B. Charlton, *Shakespearian Comedy* (London, 1938); Alvin Kernan, *The Cankered Muse: Satire of the English Renaissance* (New Haven: Yale University Press, 1959); and Robert C. Elliott, *The Power of Satire* (Princeton, N.J.: Princeton University Press, 1960).

4. G. Wilson Knight, *The Wheel of Fire* (London: Oxford University Press, 1930); D. A. Traversi, "'Troilus and Cressida'," *Scrutiny*, 7:301–319 (December 1938); L. C. Knights, "'Troilus and Cressida' Again," *Scrutiny*, 18:144–157 (Autumn 1951); Albert Gérard, "Meaning and Structure in *Troilus and Cressida*," *ES*, 40: 144–157 (1959); David C. Kaula, "Will and Reason in *Troilus and Cressida*," *SQ*, 12:271–283 (Summer 1961); Richard C. Harrier, "Troilus Divided," *Studies in the English Renaissance Drama* (ed. J. W. Bennett, *et al.*, New York: New York University Press, 1959), pp. 142–156; and A. S. Knowland, "*Troilus and Cressida*," *SQ*, 10:353–365 (Summer 1959).

5. Allardyce Nicoll, "What Do We Do With Shakespeare?" *Shakespeare Jahrbuch*, 96:35–46 (1960).

6. A. H. Scouten, "The Increase in Popularity of Shakespeare's Plays in the 18th Century," *SQ*, 7:193–194 (Spring 1956), charts.

7. *A New Variorum Edition of Shakespeare: Troilus and Cressida*, ed. H. N. Hillebrand and T. W. Baldwin (Philadelphia: J. B. Lippincott & Co., 1953). Hereafter cited only as *Variorum*.

8. See Daniel Seltzer, "Introduction," *Troilus and Cressida*, ed. Seltzer (The Signet Classic Shakespeare, New York, 1963), pp. xxviii–xxxii, for a perceptive analysis of the problems which a director must face when preparing a production of the play.

9. C. F. Tucker Brooke, "Shakespeare's Study in Culture and Anarchy," *The Yale Review*, 17:571–577 (April 1928); G. B. Harrison, *Shakespeare At Work, 1592–1603* (Ann Arbor: University of

Michigan Press, 1958); and Paul N. Siegel, *Shakespearean Tragedy and the Elizabethan Compromise* (New York: New York University Press, 1957).

Chapter II. The Theatrical Origins of the Play

1. See E. K. Chambers, *Elizabethan Stage* (4 vols., Oxford: Clarendon Press, 1923), II, 398–441, passim; and Bernard Beckerman, *Shakespeare at the Globe: 1599–1609* (New York: Macmillan, 1962), pp. ix–xvi, and 1–23.

2. See Alvin Kernan, "John Marston's Play *Histrio-mastix*," *MLQ*, 19:134–140 (June 1958), for the argument that the play is Marston's and is a unified whole.

3. Alfred Harbage, *Shakespeare and the Rival Traditions* (New York: Macmillan, 1952), p. 90; see pp. 90–119 for a full discussion of the *Poetomachia*.

4. See Beckerman, *Shakespeare at the Globe: 1599–1609*, pp. ix–xvi, and 1–23, and John J. Enck, "The Peace of the Poetomachia," *PMLA*, 77:386–396 (September 1962) for excellent accounts of the competitive, experimental nature of drama at the turn of the century.

5. See Clifford Leech, "Shakespeare's Prologues and Epilogues," *Studies in Honor of T. W. Baldwin* (ed. D. C. Allen, Urbana: University of Illinois Press, 1960), pp. 136–149, for a discussion of the rise in incidence of prologues and epilogues at the turn of the century both in general and with particular regard to Shakespeare.

6. C. H. Herford and Percy Simpson, ed., *Ben Jonson* (11 vols., Oxford: Clarendon Press, 1925–1952), I, 335.

7. I have restored the Quarto reading of "God."

8. For a full description of the vogue and its origins, see O. J. Campbell, *Comicall Satyre and Shakespeare's* TROILUS AND CRESSIDA (San Marino, Calif.: Huntington Library Publications, 1938), pp. 15–53; A. Davenport, "The Quarrel of the Satirists," *MLR*, 37:123–130 (April 1942); Alvin Kernan, *The Cankered Muse: Satire of the English Renaissance* (New Haven: Yale University Press, 1959), pp. 81–140; J. B. Leishman, ed., *The Three Parnassus Plays* (London: Nicholson & Watson, 1949), pp. 41–60, 82–92; Hallett Smith, *Elizabethan Poetry* (Cambridge, Mass.: Harvard University Press, 1952), pp. 194–256; and C. S. Lewis, *English Literature in the Sixteenth Century* (Oxford: Oxford University Press, 1954), pp. 468–478.

9. See O. J. Campbell, "Jaques," *Huntington Library Bulletin*, 8:71–102 (October 1935), and Kernan, *The Cankered Muse*, pp. 132–134.

10. See Smith, *Elizabethan Poetry*, pp. 247–253, and Kernan, *The Cankered Muse*, pp. 141–191.

11. O. J. Campbell, *Shakespeare's Satire* (Oxford: Oxford University Press, 1943), pp. 56–64, passim; *Comicall Satyre*, pp. 1–15, 54–184; and Kernan, *The Cankered Muse*, pp. 137–164.

12. In contrast see William Green, *Shakespeare's Merry Wives of Windsor* (Princeton, N.J.: Princeton University Press, 1962), for the argument in favor of a 1597 date for *Merry Wives*.

13. See Paul Mueschke and Jeannette Fleisher, "Jonsonian Elements in the Comic Underplot of *Twelfth Night*," PMLA, 48:722–740 (September 1933) and Milton Crane, "*Twelfth Night* and Shakespearian Comedy," *SQ*, 6:1–8 (Winter 1955).

14. See G. E. Bentley, "Shakespeare and the Blackfriars Theatre," *Shakespeare Survey I* (1948), 38–50, and Beckerman, *Shakespeare at the Globe: 1599–1609*, pp. vii–xii, and 13–14, for reviews of the facts about the financial interests of the Chamberlain's (King's) Men in Blackfriars.

15. W. W. Greg, *A Bibliography of the English Printed Drama* (4 vols., London: Bibliographical Society, 1939–1959), I, 18.

16. Greg, *A Bibliography of the English Printed Drama*, I, 25.

17. See T. W. Baldwin, *Variorum*, pp. 357–358.

18. C. J. Sisson, *The Library* (5th series), 15:8–20 (March 1960).

19. R. H. Barker, *Thomas Middleton* (New York: Columbia University Press, 1958), p. 10. See also p. 159, and R. C. Bald, "The Chronology of Middleton's Plays," *MLR*, 32:36 (January 1937).

20. See E. K. Chambers, *The Elizabethan Stage*, III, 366. *Satiromastix* was entered for publication on 11 November 1601; *Poetaster* with its "Apologeticall Dialogue," 21 December 1601.

21. A. F. Potts, "*Cynthia's Revels, Poetaster*, and *Troilus and Cressida*," *SQ*, 5:297 (Summer 1954).

22. See John J. Enck, "The Peace of the Poetomachia," *PMLA*, 77:393–394 (September 1962).

23. In contrast see William Elton, "Shakespeare's Portrait of Ajax in *Troilus and Cressida*," *PMLA*, 63:744–748 (June 1948), but see also Marjorie L. Reyburn, "New Facts and Theories about the Parnassus Plays," *PMLA*, 74:325–335 (September 1959).

24. Peter Alexander, "*Troilus and Cressida*, 1609," *The Library* (4th series), 9:267–286 (December 1928).

25. Harbage, *Shakespeare and the Rival Traditions*, p. 116, and T. W. Baldwin, *Variorum*, pp. 346–357.

26. See Beckerman, *Shakespeare at the Globe: 1599–1609*, pp. 15–23, for a reminder of the commercial pressures placed upon the various companies and for a suggestion of how much each play ideally should gross in order for a company to show a profit.

27. See Robert Kimbrough, "The Origins of *Troilus and Cressida*: Stage, Quarto, and Folio," *PMLA*, 77:197–198 (June 1962) for an account of the dramatic tastes of the Inns.

28. See Charlton Hinman, *The Printing and Proof-Reading of the First Folio of Shakespeare* (2 vols., Oxford: Clarendon Press, 1963), W. W. Greg, *Shakespeare's First Folio* (Oxford: Clarendon Press, 1955), and Kimbrough, "The Origins of *Troilus and Cressida*: Stage, Quarto, and Folio," *PMLA*, 77:194–199 (June 1962).

29 W. W. Greg, *The Editorial Problem in Shakespeare* (Oxford: Clarendon Press, 1942, 1951), p. xxiv.

30. Harbage, *Shakespeare and the Rival Traditions*, p. 117. See also W. W. Lawrence, "Troilus, Cressida, and Thersites," *MLR*, 37: 436 (October 1942).

Chapter III. The Literary Origins: The "Matter of Troy"

1. E. K. Chambers, *William Shakespeare: A Study of Facts and Problems* (2 vols., Oxford: Clarendon Press, 1930), I, 447–448. The *Variorum*, pp. 419–499, has a useful appendix on the problem of the sources of the play, and R. K. Presson, *Shakespeare's* TROILUS AND CRESSIDA & *The Legends of Troy* (Madison: University of Wisconsin Press, 1953), presents a detailed analysis of the play through Shakespeare's probable sources.

2. *Henslowe's Diary*, ed. W. W. Greg (2 vols., London, 1904–1908), I, 42, 109; *Henslowe Papers*, ed. W. W. Greg (London, 1907), pp. 142, 144.

3. See J. S. P. Tatlock, "The Siege of Troy in Elizabethan Literature, Especially in Shakespeare and Heywood," *PMLA*, 30:676–678 (December 1915) for a full list of plays presented in the 1590's which may have dealt with the legend of Troy.

4. Tatlock, "The Siege of Troy," *PMLA*, 30:673 (December 1915).

5. For accounts of the "historicity" of *Troilus and Cressida*, see Hardin Craig, *The Enchanted Glass: The Elizabethan Mind in Literature* (Oxford: Blackwell, 1935, 1952), p. 214, and Alfred Harbage, *As They Liked It: An Essay on Shakespeare and Morality* (New York: Macmillan, 1947), p. 124.

6. M. C. Bradbrook, "What Shakespeare Did to Chaucer's *Troilus and Criseyde*," *SQ*, 9:313 (Summer 1958). Other interesting comparisons of Chaucer and Shakespeare are H. H. Herdman, Jr., "The 'Troilus and Cressida' of Chaucer and of Shakspere," *Sewanee Review*, 7:161–181 (April 1899), and E. C. Pettet, *Shakespeare and the Romance Tradition* (London: Staples Press, 1949), pp. 140–153.

7. H. E. Rollins, "The Troilus-Cressida Story from Chaucer to Shakespeare," *PMLA*, 32:383–429 (September 1917).

8. Tatlock, "The Siege of Troy," *PMLA*, 30:760 (December 1915).

9. See N. E. Griffin, "Un-Homeric Elements in the Medieval Story of Troy," *JEGP*, 7:32–52 (January 1908) for a discussion of the respective partisan work of Dictys and Dares.

10. Douglas Bush, *Mythology and the Renaissance Tradition* (Minneapolis: University of Minnesota Press, 1932), p. 33.

11. Harry Levin, "An Explication of the Player's Speech," *Kenyon Review*, 12:288 (Spring 1950).

12. C. H. Herford, "*Troilus and Cressida* and *Euphues, His Censure to Philautus*," *Transactions of the New Shakspere Society, 1887* (2 vols., London, 1887–1888), II, 186–190; Kenneth Muir, "Greene and *Troilus and Cressida*," *N & Q* (n.s.), 2:141–142 (April 1955); and Virgil Whitaker, ed., *Troilus and Cressida* (The Pelican Shakespeare, Baltimore, 1958), p. 17.

13. See Donald Smalley, "The Ethical Bias of Chapman's *Homer*," *SP*, 36:169–191 (April 1939); Phyllis B. Bartlett, "The Heroes of Chapman's Homer," *RES*, 17:257–280 (July 1941); and Hallett Smith, *Elizabethan Poetry* (Cambridge, Mass.: Harvard University Press, 1952), pp. 303–312.

14. Presson, *Shakespeare's* TROILUS AND CRESSIDA *& The Legends of Troy*, pp. 141. In contrast, see E. M. W. Tillyard, *Shakespeare's Problem Plays* (London: Chatto & Windus, 1950), pp. 34–35, and Alice Walker, ed., *Troilus and Cressida* (The New Cambridge Shakespeare, Cambridge, England: Cambridge University Press, 1957), p. xiii, who find no convincing evidence in the play which indicates that Shakespeare used Chapman's Homer.

15. See *Rhetores Latini*, ed. Karl von Halm (Leipzig, 1863), p. 588.

16. T. W. Baldwin, *William Shakspere's Small Latine & Lesse Greeke* (2 vols., Urbana: University of Illinois Press, 1944), I, 89, and II, 239–240.

17. See Tillyard, *Shakespeare's Problem Plays*, pp. 38–44, for a persuasive commentary concerning the general influence of Lydgate on Shakespeare and the play.

18. J. S. P. Tatlock, "The Chief Problem in Shakespeare," *Sewanee Review*, 24:134–135 (April 1916); G. L. Kittredge, ed., *The Complete Works of Shakespeare* (Boston: Ginn and Company, 1936), pp. 879–880.

19. Peter J. Seng, "The Dramatic Function of the Songs in Shakespeare's Plays: A Variorum Edition" (2 vols., unpub. diss., Harvard, 1955), I, 457.

20. See S. L. Bethell, *Shakespeare and the Popular Dramatic Tradition* (London: P. S. King and Staples, 1944, 1948), pp. 180–189, for a review of the diverse estimates of Shakespeare's intention in this speech. Important additions to Bethell's review are J. M. Nosworthy, "The Bleeding Captain Scene in *Macbeth*," *RES*, 32:126–130 (April 1946); Levin, "An Explication of the Player's Speech," *Kenyon Review*, 12:273–296 (Spring 1950); Kristian Smidt, "Notes on 'Hamlet,'" *ES*, 31:136–141 (August 1950); and Alfred Harbage, *Shakespeare and the Rival Traditions* (New York: Macmillan, 1952), pp. 292–294.

21. See Harbage, "The Rival Repertories," *Shakespeare and the Rival Traditions*, pp. 58–89.

Chapter IV. The Plot of the Play and the Problem of Structure

1. T. W. Baldwin, "Structural Analysis," *Variorum*, pp. 450–454.

2. Alice Walker, ed., *Troilus and Cressida* (The New Cambridge Shakespeare, Cambridge, England: Cambridge University Press, 1957), p. xxxi. See also E. Davis, "*Troilus and Cressida*," *English Studies in Africa*, 1:21 (March 1958).

3. L. C. Knights, "'Troilus and Cressida' Again," *Scrutiny*, 18:154 (Autumn 1951); H. N. Hillebrand, *Variorum*, p. 367.

4. F. W. Sternfeld, "*Troilus and Cressida*: Music for the Play," *English Institute Essays, 1952* (ed. A. S. Downer, New York, 1954), p. 131; see also Sydney Beck, "'Broken Music' Made Whole Again," *Bulletin of the New York Public Library*, 63:487–501 (October 1959),

and Peter J. Seng, "The Dramatic Function of the Songs in Shakespeare's Plays" (2 vols., unpub. diss., Harvard, 1955), I, 450–452, for commentaries on the "fetid" moral atmosphere of the song, the scene, and the play.

5. F. P. Wilson, *Elizabethan and Jacobean* (Oxford: Clarendon Press, 1945), p. 115.

6. See Robert Ornstein, *The Moral Vision of Jacobean Tragedy* (Madison: University of Wisconsin Press, 1960), p. 245, and R. A. Foakes, " 'Troilus and Cressida' Reconsidered," *Toronto Quarterly*, 32:143 (January 1963) for excellent character sketches.

7. Harold S. Wilson, *On the Design of Shakespearean Tragedy* (Toronto: University of Toronto Press, 1957), p. 129.

8. See Theodore Spencer, *Shakespeare and the Nature of Man* (New York: Macmillan, 1942, 1955), pp. 117–121, and E. M. W. Tillyard, *Shakespeare's Problem Plays* (London: Chatto & Windus, 1950), pp. 76–80, for fine discussions of this scene.

9. See T. M. Parrott, *Shakespearean Comedy* (New York: Oxford University Press, 1949), p. 344, for an affirmation of the integrity of the battle scene.

10. See James E. Phillips, *The State in Shakespeare's Greek and Roman Plays* (New York: Columbia University Press, 1940), p. 126, for a discussion of the inconclusive nature of the end of the Greek story.

11. Alfred Harbage, *Shakespeare and the Rival Traditions* (New York: Macmillan, 1952), p. 117.

12. W. W. Lawrence, *Shakespeare's Problem Comedies* (New York: Macmillan, 1931), p. 166.

13. Lawrence, *Shakespeare's Problem Comedies*, p. 169.

14. See L. G. Salingar, "The Design of *Twelfth Night*," *SQ*, 9:117–139 (Spring 1958).

15. See Hugh Dickinson, "The Reformation of Prince Hal," *SQ*, 12:33–46 (Winter 1961) for an excellent discussion of the unity and integrity of *1 Henry IV*.

16. M. C. Bradbrook, *The Growth and Structure of Elizabethan Comedy* (London: Chatto & Windus, 1955), p. 108.

17. John J. Enck, "The Peace of the Poetomachia," *PMLA*, 77:388 (September 1962).

18. Enck, "The Peace of the Poetomachia," *PMLA*, 77:390–392 (September 1962).

Chapter V. The Concerns of Love and Lust

1. See E. M. W. Tillyard, *Shakespeare's Problem Plays* (London: Chatto & Windus, 1950), pp. 52–54, for an excellent description of the effects created by the first two scenes of the play.

2. W. M. T. Nowottny, " 'Opinion' and 'Value' in *Troilus and Cressida*," *Essays in Criticism*, 4:285 (July 1954).

3. See Alfred Harbage, "Shakespeare's Ideal Man," *J. Q. Adams Memorial Studies* (ed. J. G. McManaway, *et al.*, Washington: Folger Shakespeare Library, 1948), pp. 65–80, and T. W. Baldwin, "Shakespeare's Apthonian Man," *MLN*, 65:111–112 (February 1950) for a full account of the philosophical assumptions which are perverted in Pandarus' speech.

4. See M. C. Bradbrook, "What Shakespeare Did to Chaucer's *Troilus and Criseyde*," *SQ*, 9:314 (Summer 1958) for a sensitive comparison of Chaucer's widow and Cressida.

5. See Theodore Spencer, "A Commentary on Shakespeare's 'Troilus and Cressida,' " *Studies in English Literature*, 16:14 (January 1936) for a suggestive analysis of Cressida's vapid rhyming.

6. Alfred Harbage, *Shakespeare and the Rival Traditions* (New York: Macmillan, 1952), p. 207.

7. See O. J. Campbell, *Comicall Satyre and Shakespeare's* TROILUS AND CRESSIDA (San Marino, Calif.: Huntington Library Publications, 1938), p. 212; Tillyard, *Shakespeare's Problem Plays*, pp. 46–48.

8. See W. B. C. Watkins, *Shakespeare and Spenser* (Princeton, N. J.: Princeton University Press, 1950), pp. 22–23.

9. See Arthur Symons, "Troilus and Cressida," *Harper's Monthly Magazine*, 115:662 (October 1907) for a sensitive analysis of this speech.

10. See D. A. Traversi, " 'Troilus and Cressida,' " *Scrutiny*, 7:310 (December 1938); M. R. Ridley, *William Shakespeare: A Commentary* (London: J. M. Dent & Son 1936, 1948, pp. 79–80; Swinburne, *A Study of Shakespeare* (New York, 1880), p. 202; and Olwen W. Campbell, "*Troilus and Cressida*: A Justification," *London Mercury*, 4:51 (May 1921) for realistic appraisals of Cressida's character. But see C. F. Tucker Brooke, "Shakespeare's Study in Culture and Anarchy," *Yale Review*, 17:573–574 (April 1928); and Hamill Kenny, "Shakespeare's Cressida," *Anglia*, 61:171–172 (January 1937) for noble defenses of Cressida's reputation.

11. See W. B. D. Henderson, "Shakespeare's 'Troilus and Cressida,' Yet Deeper in Its Tradition," *Essays in Dramatic Literature; The Parrott Presentation Volume* (ed. Hardin Craig, Princeton, N. J.: Princeton University Press, 1935), p. 140, for an excellent description of the lovers' parting, and Campbell, *Comicall Satyre*, pp. 213–214, for an interesting contrast of the scene with the corresponding one in *Romeo and Juliet*.

12. In contrast L. L. Schücking, *Character Problems in Shakespeare's Plays* (trans. W. H. Peters, New York: G. G. Horrap & Co., 1922), p. 55, believes that Troilus achieves manhood when he hears Aeneas' news.

13. See Karl F. Thompson, "Cressid's Diet," *N&Q* (n.s.), 3:378–379 (September 1956) for a fine, literal reading of these lines.

14. In contrast see Coleridge's *Shakespearean Criticism* (ed. T. M. Raysor, 2 vols., Cambridge, Mass.: Harvard University Press, 1951), I, 110; Tillyard, *Shakespeare's Problem Plays*, p. 80; W. R. Bowden, "The Human Shakespeare and *Troilus and Cressida*," *SQ*, 8:167–177 (Spring 1957); and Brian Morris, "The Tragic Structure of *Troilus and Cressida*," *SQ*, 10:491 (Autumn 1959).

15. See Virgil Whitaker, *Shakespeare's Use of Learning: An Inquiry into the Growth of his Mind & Art* (San Marino, Calif.: Huntington Library Publications, 1953), pp. 111–112.

16. Alfred Harbage, "Shakespeare's Ideal Man," *J. Q. Adams Memorial Studies*, p. 79.

17. T. M. Parrott, ed., *The Comedies of Chapman* (London: E. P. Dutton, 1914), pp. 894–896.

18. Campbell, *Comicall Satyre*, pp. 112, 125.

19. Campbell, *Comicall Satyre*, p. 128.

20. W. J. Olive, "Imitation of Shakespeare in Middleton's *The Family of Love*," *PQ*, 29:75–78 (January 1950).

21. A. J. Axelrad, *Un Malcontent Élizabéthain: John Marston* (Paris: Didier, 1955), p. 181.

22. Eric Partridge, *Shakespeare's Bawdy* (London, Routledge, 1947), p. 54.

23. See Robert Kimbrough, "The Problem of Thersites," *MLR*, 59:173–176 (April 1964).

24. Harbage, *Shakespeare and the Rival Traditions*, p. 219; see pp. 186–221 for a full study of the attitudes toward sexual behavior that are displayed in the public and private plays.

25. A. F. Potts, *"Cynthia's Revels, Poetaster,* and *Troilus and Cressida," SQ,* 5:297–302 (Summer 1954).

26. Campbell, *Comicall Satyre,* p. 99.

27. See John J. Enck, "The Peace of the Poetomachia," *PMLA,* 77:393–394 (September 1962).

28. M. C. Bradbrook, *Themes and Conventions of Elizabethan Tragedy* (Cambridge, England: Cambridge University Press, 1952), p. 242.

29. Harbage, *Shakespeare and the Rival Traditions,* p. 213; see also, p. 211–214.

Chapter VI. The Demands of War and Honor

1. See T. W. Baldwin, *William Shakspere's Small Latine & Lesse Greeks* (2 vols., Urbana: University of Illinois Press, 1944), I, 89, and II, 239–240, for examples of grammar school debates framed upon this topic, and Madeleine Doran, *Endeavors of Art: A Study of Form in Elizabethan Drama* (Madison: University of Wisconsin Press, 1954), pp. 310–322, for an illuminating discussion of the effect on structure of the academic debate in this and other Elizabethan plays.

2. In contrast see O. J. Campbell, *Comicall Satyre and Shakespeare's* TROILUS AND CRESSIDA (San Marino, Calif.: Huntington Library Publications, 1938), pp. 191–193; Franklin M. Dickey, *Not Wisely but too Well: Shakespeare's Love Tragedies* (San Marino, Calif.: Huntington Library Publications, 1957), pp. 138–139; and Alice Walker, ed., *Troilus and Cressida* (The New Cambridge Shakespeare, Cambridge, England: Cambridge University Press, 1957), p. xxxi.

3. A. P. Rossiter, "Troilus and Cressida," *TLS,* 8 May 1948, p. 261, suggests that Troilus' lines 198–206 ("But, worthy Hector," etc.) should come before the following lines; this transposition tends to lessen the shock of Hector's change of stance.

4. Geoffrey Bush, *Shakespeare and the Natural Condition* (Cambridge, Mass.: Harvard University Press, 1956), p. 38.

5. See also, Paul A. Jorgensen, "The 'Dastardly Treachery' of Prince John of Lancaster," *PMLA,* 76:488–492 (December 1961).

6. See E. M. W. Tillyard, *Shakespeare's Problem Plays* (London: Chatto & Windus, 1950), pp. 68–70, for an enlightening twofold comparison of Hamlet's definition of honor with Hector's actions, and of Hector's stated moral philosophy with Hamlet's action.

7. A. Arnold, "The Hector-Andromache Scene in Shakespeare's 'Troilus and Cressida,'" *MLQ*, 14:335–340 (December 1953).

8. I regret that I was not able to obtain and read Curtis Brown Watson's fine, encyclopedic *Shakespeare and the Renaissance Concept of Honor* (Princeton, N.J.: Princeton University Press, 1960) until my manuscript was in press. Nowhere, I think, do we disagree, but I should have welcomed his scholarly support for many of the conclusions reached in this chapter.

Chapter VII. The Rhetoric of Order and Disorder

1. See Alfred Hart, "Vocabularies of Shakespeare's Plays," *RES*, 19:128–140 (April 1943), and E. K. Chambers, *William Shakespeare* (2 vols., Oxford: Clarendon Press, 1930), I, 444–447.

2. In contrast see Mark Van Doren, *Shakespeare* (New York, 1939; Anchor ed., n.d.), pp. 172–173; M. A. Shaaber, "Review: A New Variorum," *SQ*, 4:180 (April 1953); O. J. Campbell, *Comicall Satyre and Shakespeare's* TROILUS AND CRESSIDA (San Marino, Calif.: Huntington Library Publications, 1938), p. 191; and Johannes Kleinstück, "Ulysses' Speech on Degree as Related to the Play of *Troilus and Cressida*," *Neophilogus*, 43:58–63 (1959).

3. See Hardin Craig, *The Enchanted Glass: The Elizabethan Mind in Literature* (Oxford: Blackwell, 1935, 1952), pp. 72–3; Theodore Spencer, *Shakespeare and the Nature of Man* (New York: Macmillan, 1942, 1955), pp. 21–28; Herschel Baker, *The Dignity of Man* (Cambridge, Mass.: Harvard University Press, 1947), pp. 223–240; and Virgil Whitaker, *Shakespeare's Use of Learning* (San Marino, Calif.: Huntington Library Publications, 1953), pp. 195–199, for excellent discussions of the significance in the Elizabethan period of the ideas expressed in Ulysses' speech.

4. Kenneth Muir, *"Troilus and Cressida," Shakespeare Survey 8* (1955), p. 35.

5. H. B. Charlton, *Shakespearian Comedy* (London, 1938), p. 238.

6. Jackson J. Campbell's Yale Shakespeare (New Haven: Yale University Press, 1956) edition of the play is one of the very few since Rowe's to retain the reading of the Quarto and Folio; however, Campbell, p. 147, provides a scurrilous annotation of "brooch." See Robert Kimbrough, "The Problem of Thersites," *MLR*, 59:173–176 (April 1964).

7. G. W. Meyer, "Order out of Chaos in Shakespeare's *Troilus and Cressida*," *Tulane Studies in English*, 4:54 (1954).

8. G. D. Willcock, "Shakespeare and Rhetoric," *Essays and Studies*, 29:58 (1943).

9. See H. H. Herdman, Jr., "The 'Troilus and Cressida' of Chaucer and of Shakspere," *Sewanee Review*, 7:175 (April 1899); J. S. P. Tatlock, "The Chief Problem in Shakespeare," *Sewanee Review*, 24:129–147 (April 1916); W. W. Lawrence, *Shakespeare's Problem Comedies* (New York: Macmillan, 1931), pp. 138–140; and Charlton, *Shakespearian Comedy*, pp. 239–241. In contrast see Robert K. Presson, *Shakespeare's* TROILUS AND CRESSIDA *&* The Legends of Troy (Madison: University of Wisconsin Press, 1953), pp. 138–142.

10. Caroline Spurgeon, *Shakespeare's Imagery* (Cambridge, Eng.: Cambridge University Press, 1935, 1958), p. 320 and Chart VII (*As You Like It* and *2 Henry IV* have the same amount of disease imagery as *Troilus*).

11. See Theodore Spencer, "The Elizabethan Malcontent," *J. Q. Adams Memorial Studies* (ed. J. G. McManaway et al., Washington: Folger Shakespeare Library, 1948), pp. 523–535, for a detailed account of the variety of malcontented types. See also E. E. Stoll, "Shakspere, Marston, and the Malcontent Type," *MP*, 3:281–303 (January 1906), and Lawrence Babb, *The Elizabethan Malady* (E. Lansing: Michigan State Press, 1951), for other important studies of Elizabethan abnormal psychology.

12. See O. J. Campbell, *Shakespeare's Satire* (Oxford: Oxford University Press, 1943), p. 153, for the suggestion that Hamlet is similar to both a psychological and a literary satiric type. Alvin Kernan, *The Cankered Muse: Satire of the English Renaissance* (New Haven: Yale University Press, 1959), pp. 243–246, and *passim*, further elaborates the literary similarity between Hamlet and Thersites.

13. See Baker, *The Dignity of Man*, pp. 301–305, for a discussion of Chapman's "fashionable" and "flamboyant" turn-of-the-century Neo-Stoicism.

14. *Sir Giles Goosecap*, IV. iii. 41–72.

15. Jonson, Induction, *Every Man out of his Humour*.

16. Willcock, *Essays and Studies*, 29:52 (1943).

17. W. W. Lawrence, "Troilus, Cressida, and Thersites," *MLR*, 37:427 (October 1942).

18. Alfred Harbage, *As They Liked It: An Essay on Shakespeare and Morality* (New York: Macmillan, 1947), pp. 85–86.

19. Madeleine Doran, *Endeavors of Art: A Study of Form in Eliz-abethan Drama* (Madison: University of Wisconsin Press, 1954), p. 317.

20. Alfred Harbage, *Shakespeare and the Rival Traditions* (New York: Macmillan, 1952), p. 116. In contrast see Kernan, *The Can-kered Muse*, pp. 14–30, 250.

21. See A. J. Axelrad, *Un Malcontent Élizabéthain: John Marston* (Paris: Didier, 1955), pp. 37–55.

22. See Spencer, "The Elizabethan Malcontent," *J. Q. Adams Memorial Studies*, pp. 530–531.

23. Campbell, *Comicall Satyre*, p. 205.

24. Kernan, *The Cankered Muse*, p. 196.

Chapter VIII. Conclusion and Epilogue

1. A. C. Bradley, *Shakespearean Tragedy* (London: Macmillan, 1904, 1929) pp. 185, 275n.

2. Virgil Whitaker, *Shakespeare's Use of Learning: An Inquiry into the Growth of his Mind and Art* (San Marino, Calif.: Hunting-ton Library Publications, 1953), p. 195.

3. Bernard Spivak, *Shakespeare and the Allegory of Evil* (New York: Columbia University Press, 1958), p. 451.

4. Arthur Symons, "Troilus and Cressida," *Harper's Monthly Magazine*, 115:659–664 (October 1907).

5. Heinrich Heine, *Heine on Shakespeare*, ed. Ida Benecke (Lon-don, 1895), pp. 42–45.

6. See J. L. Styan, *The Dark Comedy: The Development of Mod-ern Comic Tragedy* (Cambridge, England: Cambridge University Press, 1962), for a perceptive study of the origins of the Theater of the Absurd, a study which touches on *Troilus and Cressida*, but all too briefly.

7. Una Ellis-Fermor, *The Frontiers of Drama* (New York: Oxford University Press, 1945, 1946), p. 56.

8. Clifford Leech, "The 'Capability' of Shakespeare," *SQ*, 11:123–136 (Spring 1960). See also Allardyce Nicoll, "What Do We Do With Shakespeare?" *Shakespeare Jahrbuch*, 96:35–46 (1960), and Maynard Mack, "Engagement and Detachment in Shakespeare's Plays," *Essays on Shakespeare and Elizabethan Drama: In Honor of Hardin Craig* (ed. Richard Hosley, Columbia: University of Missouri Press, 1962), pp. 275–296.

INDEX